PERSONALITY AND MORALITY

PERSONALITY AND MORALITY

A Developmental Approach

By
Sister Agnes Reardon, SFCC

TBW Books • Woolwich • Maine 04579

Dedicated
to
My Mother and Father

ACKNOWLEDGMENTS

My deep appreciation goes to Dr. Joseph Wheelwright, who read and responded to my work prior to its publication. His critique of the manuscript and his recognition of its value, as well as his desire to see it published, were an unfailing source of encouragement to me. Very special thanks also go to my publisher.

So many friends have been involved in the preparation of this work that I scarcely know where to begin. First, I'd like to thank Sr. Judianne Beltz, who designed and drew the cartoons and gave so generously of her time and talent in ways too numerous to mention. Next I want to thank Kristin Cook, who drew all the other graphics and spent many hours reworking and improving upon my basic designs. I want also to express my debt of gratitude to Judy Vistica, who was an invaluable help to me in writing and editing the manuscript; Mary Ellen Ashman, who typed the final copy and handled technical aspects of the format, including the bibliography; and Marie Rogers and Evelyn DeGiosafatto, who helped with the preliminary typing.

Finally, I am grateful to all my friends and neighbors who provided behind-the-scenes support in so many different ways—especially John and Kathleen Walsh. Without their deep interest and the unfailing generosity of everyone who helped, this book would not have been possible. I am deeply indebted to all of you.

Sr. Agnes Reardon

CONTENTS

LIST OF ILLUSTRATIONS

INTRODUCTION

THE RELATIONSHIPS that have emerged among the various sciences illustrate the dynamic inter-connection between everything in the universe. It is commonplace today to hear people talking about biochemistry or astrophysics, but the gap between psychology and morality has not yet been bridged. Psychological and moral development are related processes that belong together.

This book breaks new ground in both psychology and ethics by focusing on those areas in which personal and moral growth reinforce each other; it demonstrates how the natural moral virtues facilitate personality growth by ensuring that our natural tendencies work for us and not against us. Because so many people today mistake a self-righteous approach to virtue for the real thing, they are understandably afraid that the cultivation of the virtues will cramp their style. But they are wrong; real virtue is a vital, energizing force in the human personality, and there is no such thing as one mold for everyone. Virtue isn't something that can be artificially put on from the outside — it has to grow from the inside out. Moreover, the flowering of the natural moral virtues is so intimately related to the unfolding of the human personality that it is best to begin with children and adolescents, for it is during these formative years that the foundations of personality and morality are laid.

By drawing upon Carl Jung's theory of introverted and extraverted types, I am able to show that children with contrasting personality dynamics approach moral development very differently. Jung's theory is especially well-suited for this task because it is broad and open-ended enough to include other schools of psychology. For example, his description of the introvert is based on Adlerian theory, whereas his description of the extravert is based on Freudian theory.

1

My moral-philosophical framework is Thomistic for somewhat similar reasons. In spite of the cultural and historical limitations of Thomas Aquinas, his work still provides the broadest and most comprehensive framework for integrating the psychological dimension. His treatment of the natural moral virtues not only demonstrates a more comprehensive grasp of morality than is evidenced by many modern theorists but also leaves ample room for extensive psychological interpretation. Through a scholarly work entitled *The Seven Horns of the Lamb,* Robert Brennan's interpretation of Aquinas, I have forged a link between Thomistic thought and modern psychology by translating the overly intellectual formulations of Aquinas into more psychologically dynamic and relevant language.

Although my work is based upon an in-depth analysis of personality types coupled with an intensive study of the literature, I have deliberately adopted a simple, descriptive style so that the general public can relate to it in terms of their own experience. This non-clinical, phenomenological approach also has the advantage of engaging the readers' feelings as well as their thoughts — thereby awakening deeper insights. Moreover, there is a definite progression in the work that enables readers to begin with very simple ideas and gradually work up to more complex ones.

This work is a development of Jung's theory of introvert and extravert personality types and includes the introduction of a third type, the ambivert, which is somewhat less developed than the other two. These three types or patterns of personality development refer to different ways of perceiving ourselves and others; they shouldn't be confused with a classification system or reduced to a series of stereotyped traits.

Traits have their place, but personality type refers to the underlying dynamics from which they are derived. The traits included here are only intended to provide the uninitiated reader with a more concrete picture of the personality types as he explores their dynamics for the first time; they are not to be taken as absolutes. Still, traits are sometimes more trouble than they are worth, for there is always someone who insists that he has the characteristics of all three personality types. This may be true in the sense that everyone works hard at developing adaptive traits; thus a distinction should be made between natural traits and those that are acquired. Only *natural* traits represent type dynamics.

2

That is why the traits included here must be viewed in the light of the dynamics from which they emerged — not the other way around. Moreover, it is the *interaction* among the different traits within each personality that reflects type dynamics; individual traits as such have very little significance.

In figure 1, page 4, each third of the circle represents the first phase of development during which dynamically distinct patterns of instinctual and emotional energy crystallize very differently in the introvert, extravert, and ambivert. Because these "first phase" dynamics represent the way the vital life energy most naturally flows, they are integrally tied to the definition of type. Behaviorally, these contrasting dynamics, which motivate each type so differently, are best expressed by the terms self-expression, close relationship, and independence.

Each personality type encompasses three phases of development, usually corresponding to early, middle, and late life. Since the first phase provides the foundation of the personality, it determines type. It is into this initial phase that the later phases are eventually integrated. This integration has the effect of stretching and expanding the personality so that the differences between the types become less pronounced as growth progresses.

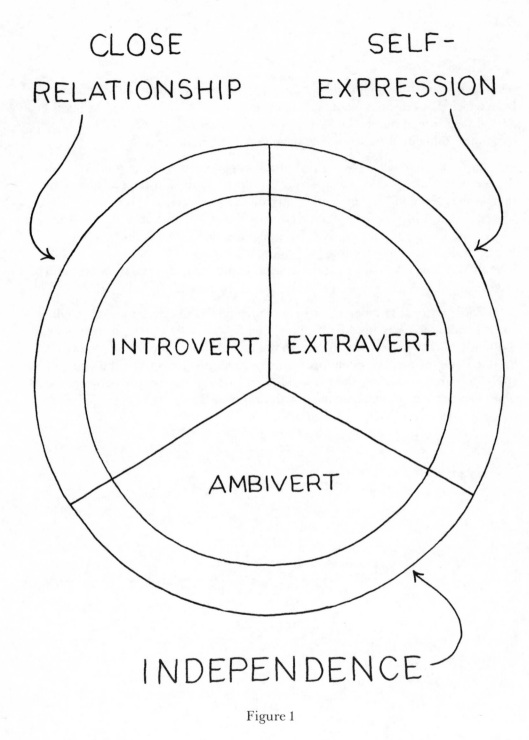

CLOSE RELATIONSHIP

SELF-EXPRESSION

INTROVERT | EXTRAVERT

AMBIVERT

INDEPENDENCE

Figure 1

4

I

PERSONALITY ROOTS IN CHILDHOOD

Extravert: Self-Expression

Extravert children are often very charming in a precocious sort of way. They are keenly aware of their instincts and emotions, and naturally want to express them; however, these instincts and emotions frequently conflict with those of their parents, and that creates a problem for them. If they don't express themselves, they get "bottled up."

Their first efforts at self-expression aren't always easy — especially at those times when their thoughts and feelings differ radically from those of their parents. They yearn for a completely harmonious relationship with their parents, but it doesn't work — at least not to their satisfaction. Because they are so aware of their own conflicting feelings and reactions, they cannot focus on pleasing their parents; extravert children experience great relief and release in *self*-expression.

Parents soon begin responding with equal candor by letting the child know exactly how they feel, and the child quickly learns how greatly his parents' reactions differ from his own. All his hopes for an undisturbed, intimate relationship are dashed upon the rocks of self-expression. He is disillusioned early and begins to move away from emotional dependence upon his parents.

Extravert children are like premature fledglings, leaving the nest of maternal nurture early and relying on their own resources before they are ready. They "toughen up" and push their desires for closeness into the background; they press onward and outward. However, they lack the foundation of emotional security that would enable them to feel really comfortable in their undertakings. Extraverts all too readily attempt more than they are capable of; they do the best

5

they can, but often fail miserably. They thrust their fears and hesitations aside and try to drown out their anxiety; as a result, they often perform tasks hastily and inadequately, leaving themselves wide open for criticism — which crushes them all the more because they are motivated by a desperate effort to win approval and recognition from their peers.

These children usually express their feelings quite freely, but often pull back when others try to help or comfort them. They sense their desire for closeness, but prefer to ignore it, fearing that close relationship would conflict with their need for self-expression. They don't want anyone to cramp their style or remind them of their fragile inner core, so they quickly dry their tears and turn to something pleasurable.

Such children need a tremendous amount of reassurance to prevent them from taking on more than they are capable of; thus they are relieved of pressure and their learning is facilitated. This reduces the restlessness of these youngsters, who are struggling to impress and gain attention in any way they can. The attention they seek is actually a substitute for the emotional support they need. Extravert children are very sensitive, but soon learn not to let hurt sink in too deeply. Brushing pain away and quickly reaching out to new experiences, they seldom waste time feeling sorry for themselves. When in trouble in a situation, they drop it and reach for a new one. Extraverts like to keep moving and learn not to take mistakes too seriously.

These children usually learn the hard way; they go through an extensive period of testing out many different people and situations. They need immediate feedback, or they will approach each new situation with the same naïveté as the previous one. Extraverts have to be stopped in their tracks while the incident is still fresh in their minds. If you wait too long to chide them, they are not likely to remember what you are talking about.

Extraverts have more energy than they know what to do with and can't be tied down to any one thing for too long; they can always be found where the action is. By the time they start school, reaching out has become a way of life for them, and the ease with which they express themselves draws many of their classmates toward them. Extraverts often say what others hardly dare think, and this has its own special charm. Mischievous and fun-loving extraverts have an instinctual vitality that refuses to be extinguished.

6

Natural Traits

An extravert: Enjoys trying new things
Is willing to take risks
Is always on the go
Spreads himself thin
Loves variety
Has many irons in the fire
Interacts with many different people
Is enthusiastic
Is spontaneous; outgoing
Is very much his "own person"
Needs space
Has too much going on inside
Feels everything immediately
Likes to act on the spur of the moment

Introvert: Close Relationship

Introvert children surrender themselves unresistingly to the womb of maternal dependence. Their deepest sense of identity is rooted in this experience of unconditional trust, and it continues to exert a strong influence on their lives, setting the stage for all future relationships. They quickly learn that striving to please their parents brings many rewards, and it gives them a sense of security that they can count on. Introverts become so adept at pleasing their parents that they bury vital and essential parts of themselves. They go beyond simple adaptation and self-control by letting many of their natural instincts be submerged.

When introverts are hurt by their parents, the pain sinks in very deeply because they have not yet discovered their own individuality; hence they absorb the pain and redouble their efforts to please and appease. When introvert children offend their parents, they often try to "make up" and apologize — without even knowing what they did wrong; they "feel sorry" because their good feelings with their parents have been disturbed. Introverts often experience their self-sacrificing love and its inevitable pain as being too deep for words.

7

These children soon learn how to make the most of every close "adult" relationship by transferring their way of relating to parents to other significant adults — without the slightest awareness of their subtle manipulations and coy maneuvers. But they soon discover that this doesn't work very well in situations with other children: other children seldom take the time to draw them out or "mother" them. Introverts are naturally shy and have to work hard at being friendly.

Introverts feel very deeply and are extremely sensitive; their feelings pervade them like the heavy atmosphere of a hazy, humid day. When you ask an introvert child what he is feeling, very often he doesn't know what to say. It takes him a long time to get in touch with specific feelings.

Whenever they plunge too rapidly into outside situations, introvert children experience a sense of confusion; they feel pulled in too many different directions at once. These children need to turn inward to get in touch with their thoughts and feelings; they must listen very carefully to what is stirring inside, or it will elude them. To discover those aspects of the world that relate to their thoughts and feelings, they turn outward; then they turn inward again to reflect and ponder on the connections.

The introvert child often feels a sense of inferiority in the presence of his extravert classmates. He realizes he isn't as popular or versatile and lacks their charm and magnetism; he secretly admires them and wishes he could be like them. The introvert realizes he's missing out on something that would make him feel much better about himself and make his life easier. His shyness makes the introvert so uncomfortable that he is forced to do something about it, so he looks for someone as shy as he is and musters up all the courage he has to reach out.

This new friendship, in which the introvert invests so much time and energy, provides him with the companionship and security that he needs in the unfamiliar world of school. The two friends depend heavily upon each other, and together they learn to cope with each new facet of school life. At first their conversation is mostly about schoolwork — something that most introverts tend to take very seriously — but gradually, if they are growing, they begin to share their *feelings* about school, too. To their surprise, the friends discover that they both feel much the same way. Knowing that they aren't alone makes accepting themselves easier; this makes them realize that their feelings are okay.

8

Because introverts are so sensitive to one another, they create an atmosphere where each can blossom and grow; each instinctively understands where the other is coming from. As a result, this awakens them to their individual needs and helps them to appreciate their individual gifts. The love and support they experience deepens their sense of self-acceptance and self-worth.

Natural Traits

The introvert: Strives to please
Is eager for acceptance
Likes to avoid conflict
Is idealistic and loyal
Is willing to sacrifice
Is always reflecting
Needs time alone
Is very sensitive
Has deep feelings
Is thoughtful and considerate
Is quiet in new situations
Is on the serious side
Is shy in large groups
Prefers a few close friends

Ambivert: Independence

The ambivert child is so naturally tuned into his surroundings and is so well-adjusted to the environment that his perception of the world and interaction with it seem to form a meaningful whole or *gestalt*. The child's experience of himself is wedded to his perception of the world, and this develops into such a stable and dependable relationship that he soon discovers something very solid and reliable in himself and finds a sense of security in the world.

Because the ambivert's experience of himself and the world, constituting a reciprocal relationship, is deeply embedded in his sensory-motor and perceptual functioning, he is provided with a natural structure upon which he can build and organize his life. Moreover, the child's awareness of himself as a vital, energizing center, serving as a clearing house for innumerable transactions and interactions with the outside world, provides him with the basis for a strong spirit of independence. As a result, his emotional investment in his parents is balanced by an equally strong investment in his own developing autonomy. Although an ambivert child strives for a good rapport with his parents, he doesn't allow them to interfere with his emerging independence.

Ambivert children are careful to observe what is appropriate and acceptable in different situations. They strive to attune themselves to what is expected of them, making an effort to fit in as smoothly as possible — without sacrificing their independence. Knowing the rules makes them feel more comfortable and secure about asserting themselves. They don't like to "rock the boat."

Common sense is basic to ambiverts; they know how to bow out of a situation gracefully without creating any ripples. When they find that circumstances no longer meet their needs, they begin to explore other alternatives and make plans accordingly. Ambiverts strive to be as self-reliant as possible. They are private people who choose to make their own decisions with a minimum of collaboration, usually having a clear idea of what they want and setting out to achieve it.

Ambiverts are so tuned into what they see, hear, touch, taste, and smell that they are more conscious of what is happening in the present than in the past or future. Their natural perceptual emphasis provides them with a fairly accurate and realistic picture of the immediate situation, and their thoughts and feelings weave themselves almost imperceptibly into the fabric of their fine-tuned sensory perception. As a result, their feelings acquire a precision that parallels their perceptual abilities. That's why ambiverts are so sure of themselves.

The hallmark of ambiverts is their natural tendency to consider all the practical ramifications of a given situation. They are seldom drawn to extremes, are rarely radical, and carefully weigh their words before they speak. Ambiverts respect existing norms and value social conventions; much of their identity is firmly anchored in established ways of doing things.

Because ambiverts straddle both sides of the circle, they participate, to some extent, in both introversion and extraversion (see figure 1, page 4). Am-

10

biverts who experience a greater attraction to self-expression are called ex-traverted ambiverts; those who are more drawn to close relationship are called introverted ambiverts.

Hence the introverted ambivert is more emotionally tied to home and parents than the extraverted ambivert, who is usually more interested in broadening his social contacts; however, the enjoyment and satisfaction that they both experience in the development of practical skills keep their desires well within bounds. Besides, they soon discover that these skills provide them with many opportunities for self-expression, and the pleasure that their parents take in their accomplishments strengthens that relationship. Their talents also earn them the respect and admiration of their classmates and pave the way for a full and rich social life.

Natural Traits

The ambivert:
Has good sense perception
Is practical; self-reliant
Is competitive; punctual
Is alert; plans ahead
Is careful about details
Likes to keep busy
Is organized; enjoys work
Values time highly
Strives to achieve
Is diplomatic and tactful
Tries to fit in and adapt
Is polite; values privacy
Seldom takes risks; is critical
Is cautious about revealing personal feelings

ILLUSTRATIONS
AND
EXPLANATIONS

RELATIONSHIP PREFERENCES

Here we see an extravert capturing the attention of a group. He channels much of his energy into making himself appealing; he "knows everybody." The extravert is welcome almost anywhere and is sure of finding someone interested in what he is doing and eager to join him.

EXTRAVERT

Here we see an introvert and a close friend upon whom she can count for almost anything. They do everything together and miss each other when they are apart. Everyone knows they are close, and no one would think of inviting one without the other.

INTROVERT

MEETING SOCIAL NEEDS

Here is an extravert who isn't afraid to tell the little fellow ahead of her to hurry up. She is thirsty, and it's natural for her to express her needs. Also, she is very much aware of the children behind her and is speaking up for their needs as well.

EXTRAVERT

INTROVERT

Here is an introvert inviting his close friend for pizza. By concentrating on the needs of his friend, he usually manages to satisfy his own needs as well. When the introvert takes his friend to lunch, he can always count on his returning the invitation.

BODY RHYTHM

Generally the extravert's body
rhythm is quick and has many
variations. Here is a little girl flip-
ping with abandon from one
handstand to the next. It's natural
for the extravert child to channel
instinctual energy with little conscious attention to each specific
movement.

EXTRAVERT

The introvert's body rhythm is
generally slower and more
studied. Here, this little boy is
consciously controlling the rhythm
of the swing; the introvert child
seems to learn specific movements
carefully before allowing them to
become fully automatic.

INTROVERT

16

WORLD VIEW

This extravert youngster is fascinated with the animals at the zoo as he moves from cage to cage, intrigued by their great diversity. He learns best by what he picks up from his wide variety of experiences and likes to get an over-all feeling for many things.

EXTRAVERT

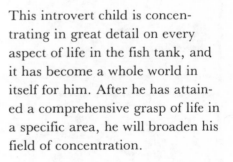

This introvert child is concentrating in great detail on every aspect of life in the fish tank, and it has become a whole world in itself for him. After he has attained a comprehensive grasp of life in a specific area, he will broaden his field of concentration.

INTROVERT

APPROACH TO LEARNING

EXTRAVERT

Here is an extravert preferring to get a feeling for the situation by getting his feet wet and plunging into the waters of experience, which gets him thinking about plans to build a bridge. The fall into the water crystallizes the energy he needs to get the project off the ground, but it isn't likely that he will take time to think the plan out in great detail before starting to build, because he prefers to figure things out as he goes along. Experience triggers thought, and thought leads directly to action—usually involving other people.

APPROACH TO LEARNING

INTROVERT

Here is an introvert preferring to get a feeling for the sea by reflecting on it first. Different ideas begin clustering around the central idea of sea that stimulate and excite her as they gradually take shape. Ideas motivate her, but she isn't likely to open herself to too many dimensions of experience at once. She emphasizes reflection so much that she tends to limit her experiential involvement — at least in the beginning — but finally, she does decide to spend a weekend at the shore. After she has taken care of all the details, she enjoys relaxing at the beach.

LENGTH OF CONCENTRATION

The extravert child often has difficulty sticking with anything too detailed for very long. Here a restless, bored little girl is wandering around the room in search of some activity. Her focus of concentration is outside herself in the world of experience.

EXTRAVERT

INTROVERT

An introvert child often has difficulty pulling herself away from whatever she is interested in. This little girl is so absorbed in her book that she doesn't realize it's time to go home. Her focus of concentration is within herself in the world of ideas.

ABSORPTION OF EXPERIENCE

This extravert is always ready to move quickly from one experience to another. Even before the assembly concludes, she is anticipating what she might do after school. Here she is asking a friend if he would like to join her for a game of tennis.

EXTRAVERT

INTROVERT

Here this introvert boy is so deeply absorbed in what was said at the assembly that he is oblivious to everything else as he leaves the auditorium. Introverts love to ponder and savor their experiences deeply for a long time afterward.

21

EXTRAVERT
LEARNING STYLE

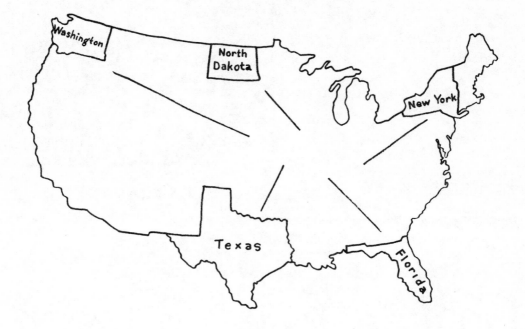

Figure 2

Figure 2. The expansive and somewhat random learning style of an extravert child is illustrated by his approach to a class project involving the study of state products. As illustrated, he begins with the most widely separated border states.

However, the first thing the extravert actually did was talk to the local grocer. *That* is what really sparked his interest. Then he began scanning many different books for clues relating to the topic: he looked for something about climate and about the transportation networks, too, gleaning whatever facts happened to strike him as he moved along. The project itself brought its own unity and organization to the many disparate facts he amassed and gave them a meaningful focus.

Initially, extravert children aren't able to focus their energies in any one direction for very long; they need to dabble here and there, to have a chance to get their bearings. Sooner or later, they find themselves pouring more energy into one project than another. Once enough experience has accumulated for them, their particular pattern of interests will emerge.

These children become impatient with knowledge that isn't directly related to experience. If the subject is biology, they'll want the specimen; if it's history, they'll be eager for a field trip. Anything theoretical or abstract has little power to hold them; they quickly become bored, preferring to go back to the "real thing"—the first-hand experience.

INTROVERT
LEARNING STYLE

ORIGINAL
TERRITORY

Figure 3

Figure 3 represents how introvert children manage to keep their focus and let everything else emerge from that center. Here, an introvert child approaches a class project on the original territory of Texas.

The original territory becomes a focus around which all the introvert's other interests begin to converge. The fact that the original boundaries don't coincide with the present boundaries of Texas doesn't phase him in the least, for he knows he will come to a deeper understanding of the present boundaries in the end. Introverts need to see how things evolve.

Everything about the original territory fascinates him. Bringing his thoughts as well as his feelings to bear on its history helps him. He absorbs it comprehensively — and no detail is considered too small to merit his attentive consideration. The introvert turns to many different source books to discover exactly what clusters of ideas he wants to explore, which interpretations most intrigue him. There is emotional energy behind his efforts.

Only after completing his study of the original territory will he expand his interest to include the surrounding states. This is similar to the way he broadens his world view, while still maintaining a central focus — that sense of a unified and harmonious whole which is so important to him. When an introvert tries to focus too much energy in widely separated areas, it goes against his natural grain, and he ends up feeling scattered and torn between competing interests without being able to see how they fit together.

EXTRAVERT
DECISION-MAKING

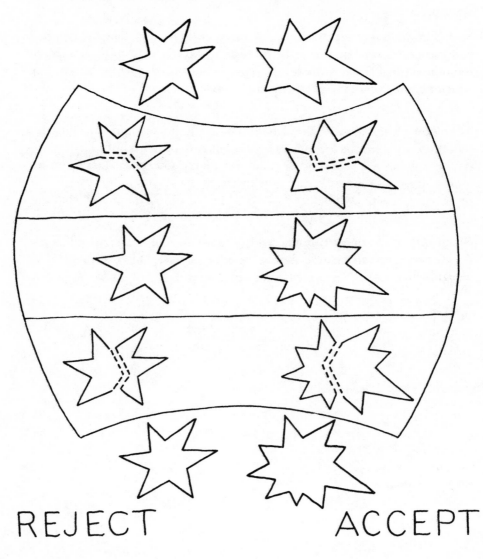

REJECT   ACCEPT

Figure 4

Figure 4 represents an extravert in the decision-making process. The starlike shapes at the top represent two situations the extravert is considering. The three divisions in the figure represent different phases of his decision-making process.

The extravert approaches decision-making from the vantage point of experience. In the first phase, he involves himself in one situation, then in the other. (The "split" stars represent the alternative approaches through which he enters the situations.)

In the second phase, the extravert tries to get an over-all perspective by stepping back somewhat, while noticing that one situation is evolving more rapidly than the other. (This is represented by the additional points on the star.)

In the third phase, the extravert takes a closer look. While keeping his eyes peeled for any significant change in the slower-moving situation, he immerses himself in the more exciting one—this time from another perspective (represented by the different angle of the split in the star). When he sees that the situation is developing favorably, he is quick to recognize its possibilities. He decides to accept it.

The extravert's choice is between two entirely different situations. The introvert's choice (see figure 5) is among the different aspects of a single situation. He is more likely to engage in an exhaustive analysis, usually concentrating on one situation at a time—in contrast to the extravert, who likes to move rapidly from one situation to the next without engaging in an in-depth analysis.

INTROVERT
DECISION-MAKING

REJECT   ACCEPT

Figure 5

Figure 5 represents the introvert in the process of decision-making. Because an introvert often experiences a sense of confusion when he plunges too rapidly into outside experience, he strives to conceptualize his experience to keep from being overwhelmed. Words help anchor his experience for future absorption and assimilation. The introvert's experience is always a bit "cloudy" until he analyzes it, taking it apart in stages, starting with the most obvious categories. Gradually the fuzzy, cloudlike mass begins to dissolve.

As different aspects begin to take on definite form, each one is examined very carefully. Instead of immersing himself in the situation, the introvert prefers to abstract from it, by formulating ideas and concepts that he can view from many different perspectives.

As his analysis progresses, it becomes increasingly refined. When the cloudiness disappears, the introvert is left with a number of concepts that he must deal with in a manageable way. Thus he arranges them in groups that best express their similarities and differences, represented by the curved and linear categories in the figure.

As a result of this "sorting-out process," the introvert will be able to intelligently involve himself in the situation in a highly selective manner. He may, for example, choose to participate only when the "curved" conditions prevail and to absent himself when the linear factors are to the fore. At the end of the analysis, the introvert has a very clear idea of those factors he accepts and those he rejects.

EXTRAVERT EXPRESSION

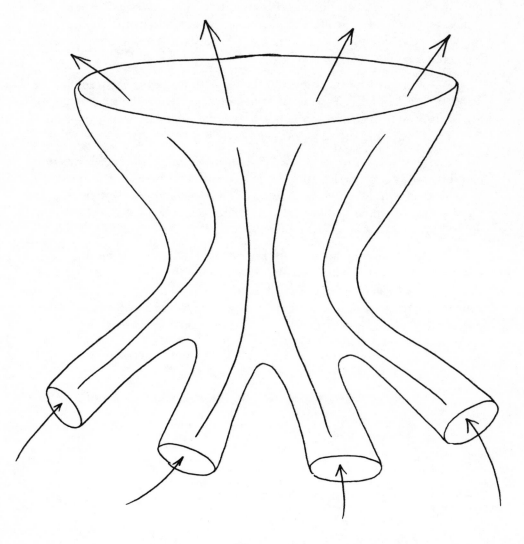

Figure 6

Figure 6 represents the extravert's free-flowing form of spontaneous self-expression. He naturally expresses his thoughts and feelings as he experiences them — while they are still registering, while they are still vibrant and alive. Moreover, his conclusions are almost always presented in descriptive terms.

The extravert's energy flows most naturally outward. He loves to immerse himself in a stream of experience and flow with it, picking up whatever happens to strike his attention as he goes along. Different aspects of situations click and register almost automatically while similarities and contrasts weave themselves almost imperceptibly into the fabric of his consciousness.

Extraverts usually "think out loud." During the course of a lively exchange, extraverts can progress through a whole series of tentative solutions. It's important that other participants recognize that the extravert is simply expressing how things strike him as the discussion moves along. Extraverts are vocal; they often express themselves with such zest and enthusiasm that they can sway an emotionally susceptible group. If no one disagrees and the extravert's conclusions are left unchallenged, their colorful and descriptive statements may prevail.

People may fail to realize that the extravert's solutions lack some essential ingredients; they may allow themselves to be carried away by an extravert's charisma. In the ideal group situation, input from all three personality types is needed because they represent three different attitudes or orientations to life.

INTROVERT EXPRESSION

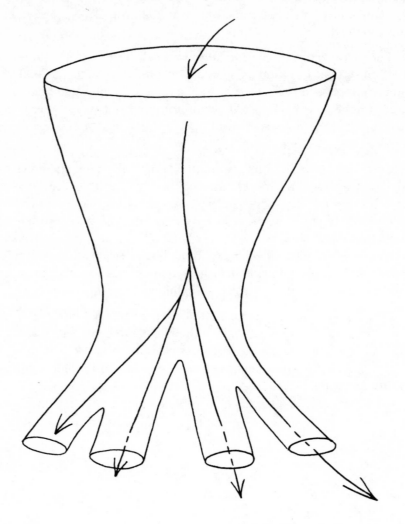

Figure 7

Figure 7 represents the introverts' approach to group discussion. First, introverts catch hold of the main theme; then they concentrate on how each point is related to that theme. During the discussion, introverts have all they can do to absorb what is being said. Because they like to examine things from every possible angle, they typically refrain from comment until after a meeting is over. That is when their real work begins.

Introverts examine each point of view very critically, noting similarities and differences, considering all the implications and ramifications. They sort out one-by-one all the half-truths, generalizations, and exaggerations. They focus on the fine points. Next they bring these insights to bear on the statements that were made and qualify the conclusions that were drawn. Then the introvert concentrates on how to present these carefully thought-out conclusions, arranging them in a persuasive order and couching them in appealing language. (This strategy is represented by the branches extending from the main line at different intervals.)

At the next meeting, the introvert waits for the most opportune moment to express himself (sometimes he waits too long and misses his chance). The introvert usually has notes to which he can refer so that everything is presented in proper sequence, and nothing is forgotten. Introverts take themselves very seriously: they want to make a significant contribution, even if it can't be done as flamboyantly as it would be done by an extravert.

If the truth be known, many introverts don't open their mouths at a meeting because they feel that what they have to say isn't perfected enough. But when they do: Beware! Those who make light of what the introvert has to say had better watch out!

EXTRAVERT
GENERAL TO PARTICULAR

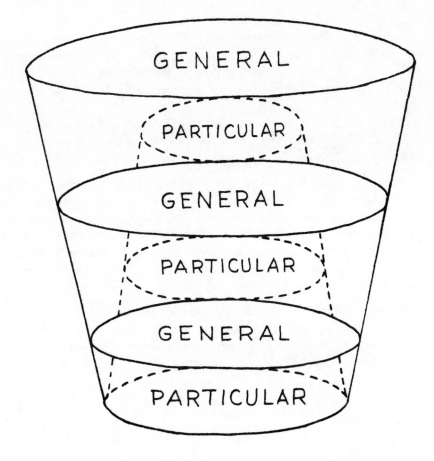

Figure 8

In figure 8 the outer vessel represents the more dominant process of extraversion; the inner cylinder represents the less dominant process of introversion.

The spheres work together in pairs with the first two spheres at the top representing the extravert's approach to learning in early life, the middle two spheres representing his approach during middle life, and the bottom two spheres, his approach in later life.

"General" refers to general experience, which is the extravert's natural teacher. "Particular" refers to the "sorting-out process," which extraverts have to work so hard at. During early life, the extravert immerses himself almost completely in experience and expends comparatively little time sorting out particulars. This emphasis gradually diminishes as he begins to focus more directly on abstraction and conceptualization in later life.

INTROVERT
PARTICULAR TO GENERAL

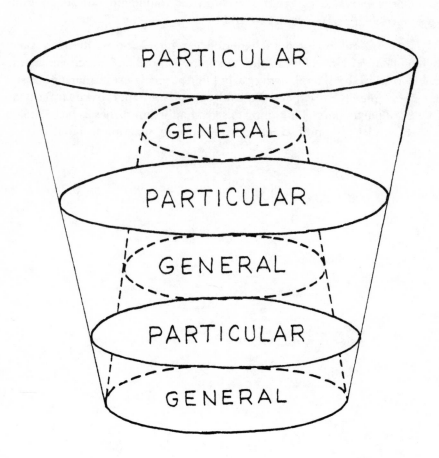

Figure 9

In figure 9 the outer vessel represents the more dominant process of introversion; the inner cylinder represents the less dominant process of extraversion.

The spheres work together in pairs with the first two spheres at the top representing the introvert's approach to learning in early life, the middle two spheres representing his approach during middle life, and the bottom two spheres, his approach in later life.

"Particular" refers to the "sorting-out process" that is the introvert's habitual approach to learning. When introverts immerse themselves in experience, they try to capture small segments of it by conceptualizing them. This emphasis gradually diminishes during middle and late life, when the introvert learns progressively more through direct experience.

Figures 8 and 9 illustrate that no one is totally extraverted or introverted.

EXTRAVERT
RELATIONSHIP

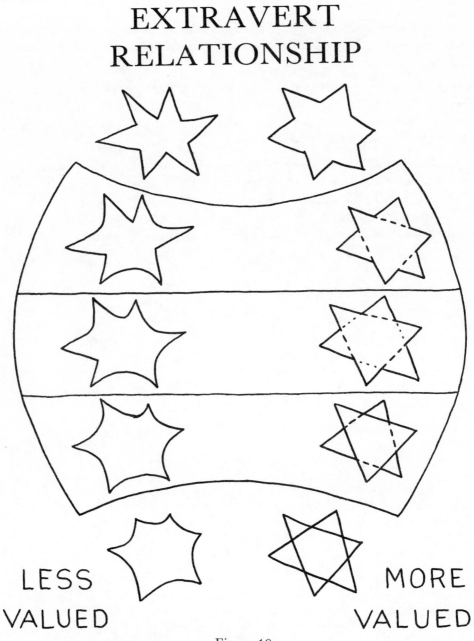

LESS
VALUED

MORE
VALUED

Figure 10

38

In figure 10 an extravert is meeting two new acquaintances (represented by the starlike shapes at the top). The lines inside the stars on the right signify a transparency that draws extraverts. The starlike shapes on the left represent a person who is more cautious and reserved; the extravert feels less comfortable with him and therefore reaches out with less confidence.

The extravert is genuinely interested, even intrigued by the reserved person, but he doesn't know how to take him, how to see behind his mask. So he bides his time, waiting for an opportunity to get to know him better (the time lag is represented by the three divisions in the figure). However, the extravert can't help being more wary of the reserved one than of the person who is so transparently open about himself.

Extraverts pay very little attention to the interplay of positive and negative qualities in a given individual. They concentrate on the positive. More often than not, they see the negative qualities but prefer to ignore them, not wanting anything to interfere with a good rapport.

INTROVERT
RELATIONSHIP

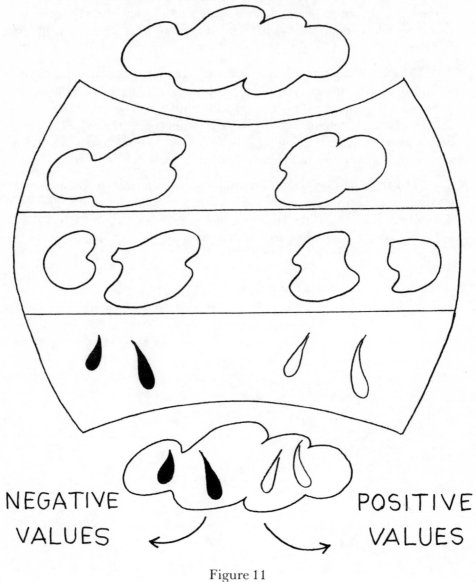

Figure 11

Figure 11 illustrates an introvert making a new friend, who is represented by the cloudlike shape at the top. He has already decided that he wants to get to know this person and has a serious interest in him.

Because introverts are so vulnerable to those they love, they have to take some precautions. Introverts have to struggle against their natural tendency to love the other *more* than they love themselves. Because introverts tend to love in a very comprehensive all-or-nothing way, they can't afford to be naive. They need to develop a critical eye in order to survive.

In this instance, the introvert concentrates almost entirely on the new friend who has become the center of his world. The two become very close, and in each new situation, they discover more about each other. Their relationship is like a crystal that can be viewed from many different angles, each side bringing new facets to light.

When they are alone together, their experience of one another is more concentrated and intense (represented by two parts of the cloud). Other aspects surface when they are at work or when they visit their families together (represented by other segments in the cloud).

The "raindrops" represent both positive and negative qualities. The introvert needs to sort out the positive from the negative qualities in order to maintain a sense of his own separate identity. Both types of qualities reappear in the cloud — signifying that the introvert loves and accepts the whole person, while at the same time making a clear distinction between his or her positive and negative qualities. This helps the introvert to remain true to himself, for he is always in danger of merging too completely with another.

KINSHIP

INTROVERT

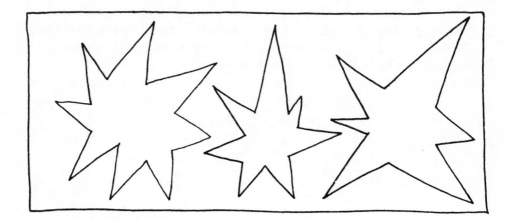

EXTRAVERT

Figure 12

In figure 12 the group of clouds represents introverts, and the cluster of stars, extraverts. The points of the stars represent the extravert's natural tendency to reach out in many different directions.

There is a strong feeling of kinship among those of the same personality type. Typically, introverts feel most naturally understood and relaxed with other introverts, while extraverts feel more comfortable with other extraverts. Each type instinctively recognizes his own.

Introverts often establish bonds among themselves for mutual support and affirmation; extraverts also band together in loosely knit groups, each instinctively respecting the territory of the other.

If you are still wondering about your own personality type, stop and think for a moment whom among your friends — excluding family — you are most at home with. Who are the people you can say almost anything to, knowing that they'll feel much the same as you? If you can identify their personality type (it's always easier to look at someone else), it's likely that you are the same.

Now stop and think of people you can never quite figure out, who always seem to have a different way of looking at things. Sometimes you feel there is no common ground between you. If they are a complete mystery to you, and you haven't the foggiest idea "what makes them tick," they are bound to be a different personality type.

43

INTROVERT &
EXTRAVERT

ATTRACT

REPEL

Figure 13

Figure 13 illustrates that relationships between introverts and extraverts are rarely neutral; most often, they are either strongly attracted to one another or strongly repelled. The strongest reactions are most likely to occur during adolescence and at other transitional stages of development. Such extremes seldom occur between persons of the same personality type—at least not with the same degree of intensity.

Extraverts and introverts touch each other's unconscious. What lies in the unconscious of the introvert is part of the extravert's conscious experience; what lies in the unconscious of the extravert is part of the introvert's conscious experience.

Extraverts and introverts are like opposite poles of a magnet. A "mysterious something" attracts, fascinates, charms, and excites polar opposites, but if the relationship doesn't get off on the right foot or takes a bad turn, this mysterious something can become very threatening and create tension.

EXTRAVERT
PSYCHIC ENERGY

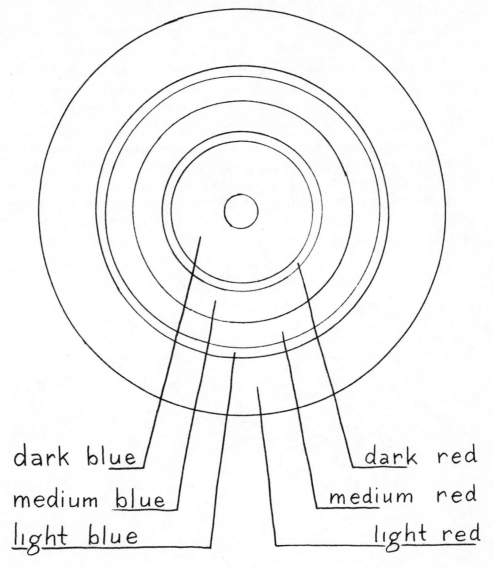

dark blue

medium blue

light blue

dark red

medium red

light red

Figure 14

Figure 14 illustrates the way psychic energy is channeled and absorbed during the extravert's life cycle. This psychic energy is the vital life energy that motivates and energizes the personality. The red and blue rings operate in pairs. The two outer rings represent the first phase of growth, the middle two represent the second phase, and the inner rings, the third phase. These three phases are roughly equivalent to early, middle, and late life; so when we speak of the first phase — as we are now — we can assume that the other two phases are not yet conscious.

The width of the rings represents a quantitative dimension; the color, a qualitative dimension. The different shades of red represent changes that occur in depth and intensity of emotional experience during a person's life cycle. The different shades of blue represent modifications in the way feelings and emotions are channeled and absorbed.

For example, in the first phase of development (represented by the two outer rings), the light red represents the extravert's natural flow of expansive energy reaching out to many different people. The thickness of the ring represents the large quantity of that energy that is available to the extravert.

The second light blue ring represents the extravert's emotional shock absorbers; its narrowness indicates the rapidity with which an extravert experiences an emotional impact. The light blue color indicates a shallow, relatively unabsorbent quality because the extravert's shock absorbers do relatively little to offset the impact of emotional stress before touching upon the third ring of more intense emotional experience.

47

EXTRAVERT

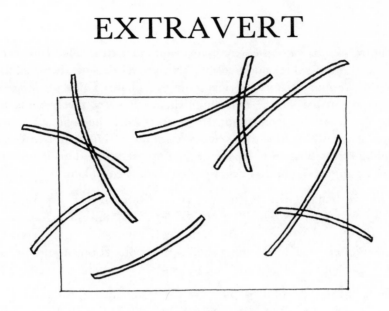

DISPERSING

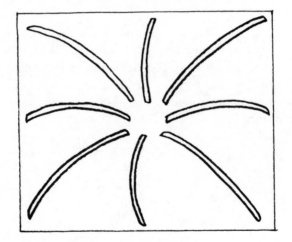

EXPANDING

Figure 15

Figure 15 illustrates what happens when an extravert touches on the third ring of the psychic energy circle (see figure 14). This third, medium red ring represents part of the second phase of development. If the extravert is not ready for this second phase, he instinctively pulls back because there is very little to protect him from the impact of raw experience. He quickly shifts gears and swings back to the outer ring of the psychic energy circle where he feels more comfortable. This is a natural reaction for the first phase of development, which results in the generally expansive, outgoing characteristics of the extravert. But when the extravert restricts himself entirely to the outer ring in an effort to avoid the beckoning of the second stage of development, dispersion results, and he becomes scattered as experience begins piling on top of experience.

INTROVERT
PSYCHIC ENERGY

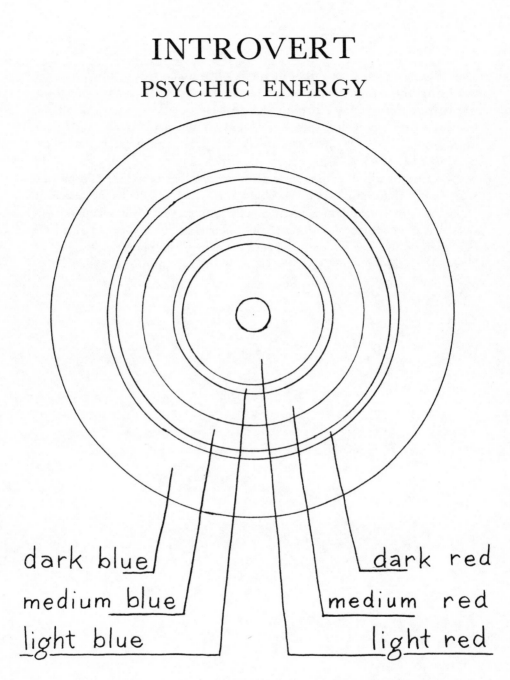

dark blue

medium blue

light blue

dark red

medium red

light red

Figure 16

Figure 16 illustrates the way psychic energy is channeled and absorbed during the introvert's life cycle. The dark blue outer ring represents the strength of the introvert's shock absorbers, and the thickness of the ring represents the relatively long time it takes for the impact of raw experience to reach him.

The dark outer ring is like a buffer that numbs and cushions the introvert from the full impact of the deep emotional intensity emitted by the dark red rays of the second ring. This outer ring is like a thick wall protecting the introvert from these intense rays by binding his energy in the intricate sorting-out process already discussed. A whole crew of deep sea divers is needed to retrieve the buried treasures of emotional experience.

The relationship between the introvert's emotional energy and the introvert's ability to absorb it is analogous to the specific gravity of a sinking object. A small object, if it is heavy enough, will sink in deep water. "Small and heavy" corresponds to the introvert's highly concentrated emotional energy (represented by the narrow, dark red ring); the deep water corresponds to the depth at which the introvert absorbs this energy (represented by the thick, dark blue ring).

On the other hand, a large object, if it is light enough, will float on water's surface. "Large and light" corresponds to the extravert's expansive energy; floating corresponds to his natural surface absorption.

INTROVERT

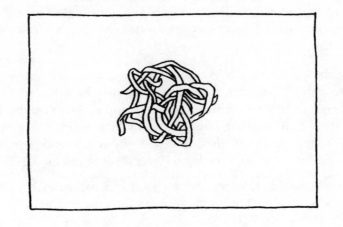

CONSTRICTING

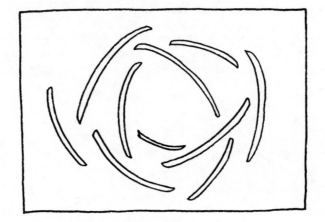

CONVERGING

Figure 17

In figure 17, notice the difference between "constricting" (cramped emotions) and "converging" (emotional integration). Constriction occurs when the introvert stays on the far edge of the outer dark blue ring so that none of the dark red rays of the deepest emotional involvement in the second ring can reach him. If the concentrated emotional energy of the second ring is approached gradually, the introvert will be able to pass through it unscathed. But some introverts, fearing their own emotional intensity, stay as far away from it as possible.

Should this happen, the introvert's natural rhythm is constricted. Feeling empty, the introvert tightens up, and all his vital life energy is squeezed out. He turns in on himself, and even his natural sorting-out process becomes a dead end. Because he is tied up in knots, the introvert needs to awaken his feelings and become involved in life once more.

II

BEGINNINGS OF MORAL DEVELOPMENT

EVERY INFANT is born into the world with the ingredients of his personality submerged in the darkness of "original chaos." Each is tossed about on the surging waves of his instincts and emotions. The parents' first task is to provide enough love and security so that the original chaos of infancy can begin to subside, and the child's personality can develop. To help the child channel instinctual and emotional energy appropriately is their next task. The child, therefore, depends on his parents for this direction and is, to a great extent, conditioned by their expressions of approval and disapproval.

It's important that parents don't completely stifle or thwart the child's instincts and emotions, for they are a mixture of good and bad; instincts and emotions are the raw material out of which the child's personality and character develop. If the child is to feel good about himself, he needs to know that his instincts and emotions are valuable because they constitute his most fundamental experience of himself.

Most people have heard of the terrible two's — the age when the child dares to say "no" and begins to revel in his experience of himself as a separate person. The sheer joy of this discovery makes him difficult to handle; consequently, wise parents learn to present the child with choices so that he can grow in his experience of separateness while continuing to respect and obey their authority.

This sense of individuality needs to be nurtured and developed for without it the child has no real basis for self-control. Notice the word "self," not "other," is linked with control. A rigid and robot-like obedience is not to be encouraged because such obedience is not sufficiently rooted in the child's experience of himself. Nor should the child be left completely at the mercy of his instincts and

55

emotions, or his emerging consciousness will be swamped, and he will be carried to a place where he doesn't want to be. This creates anxiety and fosters a sense of insecurity. The child needs to learn what it's like to be in the driver's seat and to enjoy the feeling of being in charge of himself.

But this doesn't happen all at once. Every parent knows how distraught a child in a temper tantrum can get. The youngster is driven by the sheer momentum of his own inner turmoil because he can't distinguish between the chaotic mixture of good and bad that takes possession of him. At such times parents should intervene to help the child gain control of himself. The manner in which they do this will serve as a model for the way the child will learn to deal with himself, and subsequently with others.

The child has to get a sense of how to channel his own instincts and emotions; he has to learn just how far he can let them carry him. When setting boundaries, parents should be flexible enough to allow him to discover the ebb and flow of his rhythm between impulse and control. Self-control shouldn't destroy this natural flow; rather, it should channel it in constructive directions. If parents have a sense of the child's struggle to find his own rhythm, they can help him.

This task becomes easier if parents realize that instinctual and emotional energy is channeled very differently in children of different personality types. Extravert children are in danger of letting their instinctual and emotional energy carry them away; they need to right the balance by learning how to master their own rhythm of impulse and control, much like a young musician learning to play a musical composition. Introvert children have a very different problem. They tend to stifle their instincts and emotions, becoming too fearful and hesitant. They need to right the balance by learning how to trust their instincts and emotions; too much emphasis on self-control inhibits them even more. Without realizing it, parents sometimes reinforce these inhibitions in such "model" children. Introvert and extravert children have very different tasks—both need to move in the direction that will help them to find their natural rhythm.

The development of the natural virtues helps the child to build on his natural tendencies. However, building on natural tendencies is good only up to a certain—often predictable—point. For example, it would be a mistake for a naturally hesitant and cautious introvert to emphasize patience to the exclusion of courage. This is why we can't even begin to talk about virtue apart from personality dynamics. However, because many people mistake a caricature of virtue for the real thing, they feel that everything vital, natural, and energizing is bound to be stifled or even destroyed in the process of developing the natural moral virtues. This is unfortunate because real virtue is a dynamic force in the personality. It isn't something static that can be artificially put on or imposed from the outside, and there is no such thing as one mold for everyone.

Justice, fortitude, prudence, and temperance (parent virtues from which all others derive) establish the child's personality on a solid foundation by ensuring that his natural tendencies work for him and not against him. They help the child to eliminate the destructive aspects of his original chaos, and to bring out his positive qualities. There is no reason why virtue should be approached negatively; the development of the natural moral virtues contributes to a happy and successful life. Virtue is one of the first and absolutely essential steps in spiritual development because there is a very real sense in which spiritual growth depends on personality and the development of its virtues.

The Dynamics of Justice

Justice is most simply defined as the decision to do what is right by everyone no matter how we feel about them. It provides us with an attitude of basic acceptance and respect for others and urges us to consider their needs and our resources; without this attitude, we would not be able to overcome our natural prejudices and narrow viewpoints. Justice paves the way for understanding and friendship with those who are different from us—whether these differences be those of race, religion, or personality type.

Aquinas described three kinds of justice: legal, distributive, and commutative. I use the word "social" in place of distributive, and the word "personal" in place of commutative. (See figure 18, over.) Personal justice has an advantage over the other two because it provides an opportunity for direct interpersonal communication. Both parties can fully discuss their needs and resources

JUSTICE

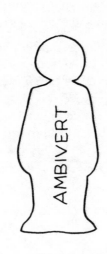

PERSONAL

LEGAL

SOCIAL

Figure 18

and reach an understanding. It serves as a model for all other forms because individual needs or problems can be taken into consideration on a one-to-one basis.

Introverts have a natural affinity for personal justice because of their preference for close relationship. Because they are so sensitive to the needs and desires of those they love, they often excel in personal justice. But introverts are not likely to value legal justice as highly as the ambivert does, nor social justice as highly as the extravert does.

Social justice usually has the strongest appeal for extraverts, who launch out into the broader society early in life expecting to find a second home there — only to discover a whole host of social evils. Too individualistic and expressive to find a haven of contentment at home, and yet not quite prepared for stepping out into a highly competitive society, many extraverts naturally gravitate to social protest movements. They frequently overlook the delicate sensitivities of personal justice to concentrate their energies on alleviating the social problems of the day, which they consider to be much more important.

The extravert develops a social conscience that is extremely critical of existing social structures and institutions that he views as contributing to social problems. He knows that grave injustices, such as slavery, were once enforced by law and supported by social conventions. He knows too that slavery contributed to the affluence of southern landowners and their descendants, some of whom are still living. Furthermore, the extravert's social conscience carries him into the future with a concern for how decisions made in the present will affect future generations; he persistently asks the question: "Are we being fair to those who will follow after us, or are we allowing our concern for the present to completely determine the decisions we make?"

For his part, the ambivert values the opportunities that present themselves in existing social structures and organizations; he learns to compete and achieve within that framework, and is more likely to stress legal justice. Legal justice emphasizes the present because the problems immediately confronting us must be dealt with in terms of existing laws, regulations, and policies. It emphasizes the importance of maintaining an established social order.

Ambiverts are opposed to anarchy; they recognize the need for stability.

They have a clear picture of the chaos and suffering that would result if the structures of social organization were to break down. Although extraverted ambiverts have strong feelings for what extraverts are saying in regard to social justice, they usually prefer to work for change by gradually weaving it into established structures. Likewise, introverted ambiverts have a strong feeling for personal justice, but seldom carry it to the same degree of sensitivity that most introverts do; their own personal independence is their main concern.

Since different personality types tend to emphasize different kinds of justice, there is a danger of focusing too exclusively on only one form of justice. Viewing justice from the vantage point of personality types helps us to widen our horizon so that we can see beyond the narrow confines of our own perspective —whether it be that of an introvert, extravert, or ambivert.

These three forms of justice are integrally related to one another, and all three need to be integrated into the human personality. In order to attain wholeness, we must leave room for the expansion of our natural tendencies so that we won't become victims of our own limited perspective. We should be careful not to mistake the natural bias of our own personality type for the whole.

Introvert children develop a sense of personal justice through their sensitivity to close relationships. Because they concentrate in such detail on the needs of those they love, their standards tend to be high. Sometimes too high. They are often more concerned about the other person than they are about themselves. This can result in resentment when others fail to respond with the same degree of sensitivity and concern. Many introvert children don't know what to do under these circumstances. Let's look at how such a struggle reveals itself in the life of an introvert child:

Jim's teacher is a very important person in his life. He strives very hard to please her and measure up to her expectations in every way he can. Thus his teacher appreciates his efforts and puts him in charge of buying extra supplies when they are needed.

One day Jim and a classmate, Mike, were assigned to work on two separate parts of the same project. Their first task was to decide on the supplies they each would need. Mike drew up his list and gave it to Jim, knowing that it was his responsibility to purchase supplies. After checking the list over with the teacher, Jim set out for the store.

Mike wasn't Jim's favorite person. Jim had tried his best to win him over, but it never seemed to work. The harder he tried to be nice, the worse things got; it was almost as if Mike were taking advantage of Jim's good will. Jim didn't know how to relate to those who were not close friends; consequently, he didn't know how to handle Mike. It weighed heavily on him.

When Jim arrived at the store, he decided to buy what he needed for his part of the project *first*. He was excited when he saw all the different supplies that could enhance his part of the project. Suddenly he got an urge to purchase the better quality items for himself and the less expensive ones for Mike. He calculated very carefully so that he could also buy some extra items for himself and still manage to get the supplies Mike had requested. In this situation Jim was reversing his normal pattern of giving more to others and being satisfied with less for himself. He was excited and a bit scared, but he decided to go through with it.

When Jim got back, Mike immediately noticed the difference in the items, but Jim pretended that nothing was amiss. He reasoned that the differences in the supplies could easily be viewed as accidental. "Anyone else would be able to get away with this," he thought. "Why not me? After all, I got everything Mike asked for . . ."

But he hadn't! All at once Mike began lashing out at Jim for having bought the best supplies for himself, and extras besides! Moreover, Jim had neglected to buy one of the items Mike had requested. Mike was angry; he slammed the door and stormed down the hall to report the incident to the teacher.

Jim was shocked. He had labored so carefully over his calculations that he could hardly believe he had overlooked one of Mike's items. He had fully intended to buy everything on the list. How could such a simple incident have gotten so out of hand! It had never occurred to him that Mike would tell the teacher.

When his teacher called Jim in, he was very upset; his face turned beet red, and he had to put all his energy into trying to control his nervousness. Jim hadn't the slightest idea of how he was going to defend himself; deep down he felt guilty, but he wasn't entirely convinced that he was in the wrong. All he could manage to say was, "I didn't realize I had forgotten the item. I don't know how I happened to overlook it." The teacher, sensing how upset Jim was, made light of

61

FORTITUDE

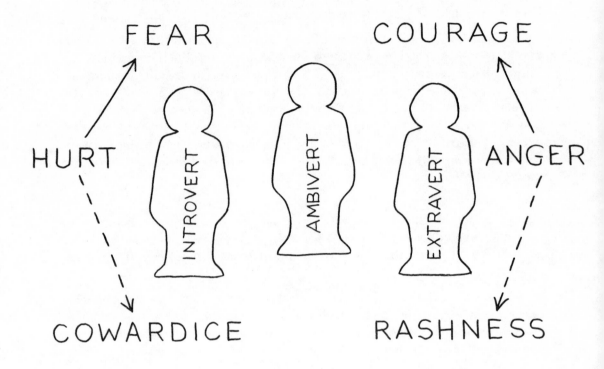

Figure 19

the matter and gave him the money to buy the missing item, without asking any further questions.

Jim was tremendously relieved. He wouldn't have known what to say if the teacher had questioned him further. He didn't know why he hadn't followed his normal pattern of getting the better items for the other person. This time he had followed an urge that seemed right to him at the moment. Why?

When Jim got home that afternoon, his mother could see that there was something wrong. "Anything special happen at school today, Jim?" she asked as she opened the refrigerator to get him a glass of milk.

"Yes," Jim answered, "there was a boy who . . ." and he recounted the entire story without ever revealing that *he* was the boy. He was sure that she'd never suspect it was he! They talked for a long time without his mother ever letting on that she knew. (Although introverts depend heavily on close relationships, they are usually very shy when it comes to expressing their feelings, especially if it might lower their image in the eyes of someone they love.)

Jim's mother questioned him about the boy who was usually "supergenerous." She wondered why he didn't want to be as fair to himself as he was to others.

"But he did," Jim insisted, "that's why he . . ." Then he stopped and thought for a moment. "I know what the boy should have done. He should have divided the money exactly in half and bought the best he could for each. He doesn't have to give others more, and he doesn't have to cheat himself either. Just be fair."

Jim's mother smiled at him. "He is fast approaching the age of reason and will soon be developing a conscience of his own," she mused.

The Dynamics of Fortitude

According to Aquinas, fortitude, or the strength to overcome obstacles, consists of a balance between courage and fear (see figure 19). Courage gives us the impetus to move against destructive obstacles, whereas fear impels us to draw back when it is appropriate — thereby resolving the conflict between the two. Courage motivates us to work at overcoming obstacles; fear keeps us from undertaking more than we are capable of.

If the connection between fear and courage seems puzzling, stop and think for a moment how gracefully predatory animals blend courage and fear while they stalk their prey. When fear alerts them to danger, they instinctively dart out of sight, while continuing to observe what is going on. Fear and courage are so smoothly co-ordinated that the rhythm of backing off and moving forward is never broken. Fear doesn't inhibit their basically courageous impulse; it merely checks it until the time is right to pounce upon their prey.

Anger is an instinctive survival reaction that alerts us to evil and energizes us to struggle against it. Anger alleviates pain while it mobilizes us for action, but it sometimes results in erratic and impulsive behavior without providing a constructive solution to the problem. Courage channels anger into constructive behavior that leads to overcoming the obstacle.

Hurt or pain signals that something is wrong. If we concentrate exclusively on the hurt without making any effort to deal with its causes, we are liable to become cowardly. Only cowards flee when they are capable of overcoming a destructive obstacle that stands in the way of some good. Cowardice transforms a healthy fear into panic; it impels us to back off and run away when action is called for. Fear triggers a realistic awareness of our limitations and of our enemy's strength. It begets a healthy caution that leads to more discriminating action.

As you might have already suspected, the introvert's struggle is usually between cowardice and fear; the extravert's between rashness and courage. Since the young introvert tends to transfer his pattern of relating to parents to other relationships, he is more likely to experience hurt than anger. As long as he directs all his energy into placating those he fears, he is not likely to become angry. Since the extravert moves away from parental dependence and opts for self-expression early in life, he is more apt to experience anger, and the fighting instinct will inevitably make its appearance whenever he finds himself up against the harsh realities of life. The ambivert engages in a struggle between the two opposing sides of consciousness, courage and fear, and usually ends up in a middle of the road position that won't jeopardize his social standing. But anger almost always surfaces before hurt, even in the introverted ambivert. Every ambivert is well acquainted with the fighting instinct and secretly wishes he could engage in an all-out battle; however, this anger is seldom expressed publicly because so much of his identity is bound up with his social image. The ambivert usually compensates for frustration in one area by making up for it in another; for example, establishing long-range goals and finding socially acceptable ways of relieving present tensions.

Now let's see how an extravert child tries to utilize those aspects of fortitude (anger and courage) that are most related to her natural tendencies. Developing natural gifts and growing in virtue are so intimately related that they can be regarded as complementary parts of a single process.

Lucy is an extravert girl with a special feeling for the social problems that face slow learners at her school. When other children make fun of them, anger surges within her. This anger gives her the courage to speak up and ask the principal if she and some of her friends could read to the slow learners during their free period each week.

The principal hesitated because he knew that all the teachers would be opposed to anything that might involve more work. But he was impressed by Lucy's enthusiasm and genuine concern for slow learners, so he promised to give her permission if she would accept responsibility for organizing the project and would see it through to the end of the year. Lucy enthusiastically agreed.

The principal gave her an official okay and appointed a teacher to oversee the project, with the understanding that Lucy would be responsible for scheduling the students and seeing that they got there each week. Lucy was excited about the project, and her enthusiasm was contagious. She and her friends enjoyed their new service roles, and the slow learners benefited from the special attention.

After a month or so, Lucy forgot to find replacements for students who were sick. A week later, she was late getting the schedule up. Before too long, the teachers began complaining that the project was more trouble than it was worth; they didn't like working with students who weren't responsible. After a series of such incidents, the principal decided to disband the project.

Lucy was upset by the principal's decision and tried to explain the reason for her slip-ups, but to no avail. She couldn't understand why her oversights were a sufficient reason to disband such a helpful project that was doing so much good. When the principal spoke to her about the teachers' feelings, she couldn't accept them as valid.

Lucy became angry when she realized that the principal's decision was final. She talked it over with her parents and tried to convince them that the principal was completely at fault. She felt that he had disbanded the group too soon without giving the students enough of a chance to prove themselves, that he didn't have enough feeling for slow learners. She also felt that he was overly sympathetic to the teachers' feelings and didn't have the courage to resist their pressure. Her parents listened to her and agreed that she might well be right in her assessment of the principal's faults, but they also pointed out that the project probably would have succeeded if it hadn't been for her oversights. Fortunately Lucy's parents were wise enough to know that if she developed the habit of placing all the blame on others, she would never learn from her own mistakes, no matter how small they were. They didn't want to see her repeat the same mistakes and fall into a cycle of repeated failures.

Her parents knew that Lucy, like many extravert children, had difficulty sticking with any one thing for too long; they knew she was inclined to be forgetful and leave loose ends for others to pick up. When her enthusiasm began to wane, her interest shifted to something else. They didn't press her to be more organized; they knew that she would have to work with her own rhythms and find her own way. Lucy didn't lack the motivation to succeed with a project. She just needed time. Her parents encouraged her to be patient with herself and to make small efforts along the way to incorporate a feeling for detail into her tasks. In the meantime, they advised her to share her responsibility for projects with someone who was naturally attentive to details.

Fear of undertaking more than she was capable of would have led Lucy to make some provision for her own limitations. She was lucky to have parents who could help her pinpoint her faults. They recognized that she had the capacity to get a project off the ground and wanted her to continue using and developing that gift.

The Dynamics of Prudence

The virtue of prudence helps us to find ways of applying principles like justice to everyday situations; it is most simply defined as good judgment in the practical application of general principles. Although prudence is grounded in thought, its goal is to bridge the gap between thought and action. Prudence is chiefly concerned with finding ways and means of putting general principles to work in concrete situations.

According to Brennan's interpretation of Aquinas, prudence involves four different ways of perceiving and reflecting: foresight, hindsight, roundsight (circumspection), and insight (see figure 20, over). Again we discover a certain affinity between personality types and the different forms of virtue — this time the virtue of prudence as it relates to justice.

Most extraverts have a vision of the way society ought to be in the future (foresight), but they spend less time considering what effect their future-oriented ideas will have on the present (roundsight) or reflecting on the effects of past history (hindsight). When it comes to a social justice issue like shutting down a nuclear power plant, young extraverts sometimes act without sufficient thought, and prudence depends on thought. Roundsight keeps the extraverts' social protest from turning into anarchy by insisting that they consider the effect of their action on existing social conditions; hindsight keeps them from repeating past mistakes.

The naturally cautious introvert usually concentrates more on learning from past experience (hindsight) than on roundsight or foresight. His tendency to hold onto the past causes him to view the present and future mainly from the perspective of past experience — a much too static view. When it comes to a personal justice issue like being cheated by a friend he wants to keep, the introvert often spends so much time considering what to say and how to say it, that the present opportunity passes him by; the longer he waits, the more awkward it becomes, and he eventually gives up. Roundsight prevents the introvert from concentrating so much on an in-depth analysis that he fails to act — it keeps him focused on the basic issue and prevents him from losing sight of it by concentrating too much on details. Foresight enables him to take an active role in determining his own future.

PRUDENCE

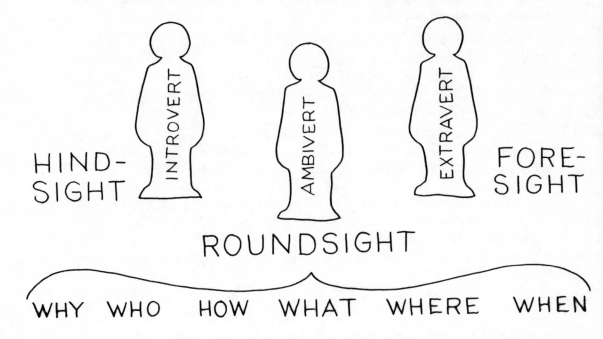

DOCILE – INSIGHT – SHREWD

HIND-SIGHT

INTROVERT

AMBIVERT

EXTRAVERT

FORE-SIGHT

ROUNDSIGHT

WHY WHO HOW WHAT WHERE WHEN

Figure 20

Ambiverts tend to view the past and future mainly from the vantage point of the present. They emphasize roundsight by focusing on the why, who, how, what, where, and when of the present situation, especially in the area of legal justice to which they are most naturally inclined. By giving them the insight to understand the principles on which laws are, or should be based, prudence keeps ambiverts from getting locked into a strictly literal approach to law. Many people think that ambiverts are the most prudent of all the personality types because they are so tuned into the practical aspects of the present situation, but this is not necessarily so. Although the awareness of different circumstances has a strong bearing on prudence, it is not the essence of the virtue; prudence depends on principles that open our eyes to what is right and wrong in a given situation. Ambiverts sometimes get so caught up in the labyrinth of bureaucratic regulations and policies that they lose sight of underlying principles.

Principles like justice, which involve the integration of personal, social, and legal dimensions, carry us beyond the limitations of our individual experience. They enable us to look at the different sides of a situation because they embrace a larger reality than we perceive at a given point in time; they prevent us from becoming victims of our own psychologically relative position in time and space.

Shrewdness and docility provide us with insight, which is an essential part of prudence. Insight enables us to break through our neat little categories of black and white by challenging us to deal with grey areas. Without insight, we would never be able to overcome our natural bias.

Docility implies a readiness to learn from others, a willingness to assume the role of a student, if you will. Some people act as if they are sufficient unto themselves and find it hard to consult with others; even when they do, they usually prefer someone who is so sympathetic to their point of view that nothing much is gained. Docility involves learning something *new,* and it challenges us to make these new ideas our own by modifying our previous attitudes. Much more is required than simply taking advice: docility requires an ability to integrate a contrasting point of view.

Introvert chldren often hold those they love in such esteem that they swallow whatever is said without digesting it — that is, without relating it to their own ideas. Docility requires a certain strength (fortitude) that keeps new ideas from completely obliterating old ones so that integration can occur. As long as introverts guard against "indigestion," they can rely on their natural affinity for docility and make rapid progress in this virtue.

Shrewdness is often mistaken for a kind of slyness or craftiness that enables us to manipulate others for our own advantage, but real shrewdness, like all the other forms of prudence, must be based on justice. The virtue of shrewdness brings us face to face with the hard facts about ourselves and others; it encourages us to overcome our naïveté about the world and the way it functions, and it keeps us from underestimating the world's influence upon us. Without shrewdness, we are in danger of looking at ourselves and others through rose-colored glasses that distort our perception and cloud our judgment. Shrewdness encourages us to find out whatever we need to know in order to keep illusion from overtaking truth. People who make judgments before all the facts are in and make decisions based on biased or misleading information are failing in shrewdness.

The naturally outgoing extravert usually takes the initiative to find out whatever he needs to know, but there is always the danger of his using the information to his own advantage, especially if he is in a tight spot. Even an extravert who espouses justice is sometimes unaware of his natural bias and ends up using information in a way that takes unfair advantage of the other person; this is all the more destructive when the other person is too naive to realize what is going on. Shrewdness has its limits when it lumps facts together in black or white categories that fail to take mitigating circumstances into consideration. That is why shrewdness needs docility to complement it. Docility enables us to discern a human face beneath the hard facts; it puts flesh and blood on the dry bones of shrewdness so that we can complete the picture by rendering judgment with an understanding heart.

Insight integrates all the different kinds of "sight" by revealing how general principles can be applied in specific situations. Foresight keeps us from being completely determined by the conditioning effect of the past and present; hindsight prevents us from living an illusory or provisional existence too geared to the future, so that we can deepen our understanding of the present. Obviously the deeper the hindsight and the more prophetic the foresight, the more creatively we can live in the present. In the example that follows, an introverted ambivert girl, Kate, focuses so exclusively on the present that other important dimensions are overlooked.

After being nominated for class president, Kate was asked to participate in a debate dealing with the pro's and con's of busing children out of neighborhood schools. During the debate, she took a strong stand against busing, claiming that it would create social and academic adjustment problems for black and white children alike; she also cited some economic considerations related to cost. Kate's participation in the debate lost her the election. What happened?

The black students were alarmed by the staunchness of Kate's convictions. She had defended the why, who, how, what, where, and when of her position in a very convincing manner, but that was precisely what infuriated them. They regarded her as dangerous because she spoke out so sincerely without any awareness of how the injustice of the past continues to influence present conditions. Kate concentrated exclusively on practical considerations, all of which were well within the bounds of legal justice, but the black students were concerned about society's responsibility to help redress past wrongs. It was Kate's lack of insight coupled with the rock-sureness and airtightness of her convictions that led them to band together and lobby against her. Indeed, Kate's opponents were so successful that they gained the support of many white students who had previously opposed busing. The black students made it clear that they weren't opposing Kate simply because she was against busing, but because she had not addressed the issue of social justice — righting past wrongs — and had not come up with any alternative solution.

Kate was shocked by their response; she felt terribly misunderstood and really couldn't comprehend what she had done to arouse so much anger. In the past she had always been fairly good at assessing situations and predicting their outcome. "What happened this time?" she wondered. How could a handful of black students manage to gain so much support, and why were they accusing her of being insensitive? Kate kept protesting that she had a genuine concern for black students and in her own way, she did, but no matter how hard she tried to convince them, it was all to no avail. She lost the election.

Parents can help ambivert children by emphasizing the importance of gaining insight into controversial issues, and by encouraging them to learn from firsthand experience. Getting involved with different kinds of people will help them gain the awareness they need to carry them beyond their present consciousness. Those with insight can take a stand against controversial issues with much more credibility than those without it, and their chances of evoking hostility are greatly diminished.

This obviously requires effort—a different kind of effort than Kate was used to. She was always looking for clear-cut answers and didn't like getting involved in the muddy waters of emotionally toned issues that confused and clouded her thinking. Parents and teachers should encourage a child like Kate to view firsthand experience as an essential part of the educational process, even though it can't be approached in the same way as a strictly academic project. Without this encouragement, an ambivert child tends to avoid such encounters because he doesn't get the same kind of satisfaction and rewards that he is used to. An ambivert naturally gravitates toward clarity; it makes him feel more secure and sure of himself.

III

ADOLESCENCE AND THE DYNAMICS OF TEMPERANCE

TEMPERANCE TONES down the excesses of our sensual nature so that its sensibilities and passions don't completely dominate our lives and obliterate the rest of our personality. Temperance doesn't annihilate or destroy our natural instincts; it enhances them by encouraging all the different facets of our personality to work harmoniously together. This virtue works *with* our natural tendencies and integrates them into the over-all structure of our personality.

Temperance is especially important during adolescence. Teen-agers need it to keep from being overwhelmed by all the instinctual and emotional changes that are taking place because adolescence is a time of extremes. Sometimes the adolescent is so talkative that you can't get him to stop; at other times he keeps completely to himself, and you can't reach him at all. Parents never know what to expect and have a hard time dealing with such unpredictable behavior. Watching the teen-ager struggle to achieve a whole new equilibrium is difficult for them; they never know whether or not to intervene at a given point in time, and if so, how.

The experience of adolescence is different for the three personality types. During this difficult period of disequilibrium and transition, extraverted feelings begin surfacing in introverts and introverted feelings in extraverts. While these contrasting feelings—so reminiscent of early childhood struggles—are seeking a new equilibrium, teen-agers frequently exaggerate the natural tendencies of their personality type in a sometimes desperate effort to retain a sense of their own identity.

Many young people today try to alleviate these growing pains by indulging in some form of escape because they don't know how to cope with the

73

TEMPERANCE

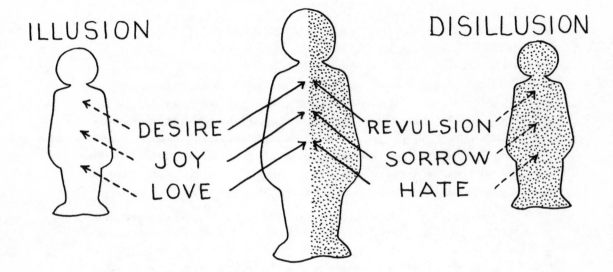

ILLUSION   DISILLUSION

DESIRE   REVULSION
JOY   SORROW
LOVE   HATE

REAL PERSON

Figure 21

physiological and psychological changes that are taking place. Instead of seeking the help they need, some of these teen-agers find an escape in drugs or alcohol, or sex. Unfortunately, habits developed during adolescence are often hard to break, and they frequently establish patterns that continue throughout adult life.

Adolescence is the time of first love, and every parent knows how full of illusion the experience of romantic love can be. In figure 21, the central image represents the beloved as he or she really is, with both positive and negative qualities. The image on the left represents the experience of falling in love, during which the adolescent typically attributes the qualities of a god or goddess to the beloved. On the right, the image represents the inevitable period of disillusionment when the idol falls and the negative aspects of the god or goddess cast a dark shadow. Temperance helps the adolescent to moderate these excessive reactions by encouraging him to love and accept people the way they are.

According to Aquinas, temperance deals with the emotions of desire and revulsion, joy and sorrow, love and hate. The tension between these polar opposites is largely due to the mixture of positive and negative qualities in the one we love. The virtue of temperance helps us to preserve a certain equilibrium in spite of our limitations, whereas intemperance side-steps the basic issue by providing a temporary escape in drugs, food, alcohol, or sexual promiscuity. Temperance enables us to accept the pain of disillusionment and frees us to love with greater maturity.

In the three descriptions of adolescence that follow, you will see that each personality type is characterized by a qualitatively different kind of struggle; the dynamics of desire and revulsion, joy and sadness, love and hate are constellated very differently in each. Although the temporary escape may be the same for all three types, the natural tendencies that motivate excesses arise from very different dynamics.

Extravert Adolescent

The extravert adolescent experiences a sharp contrast between his fragile inner core and the confident image he projects outwardly. Inwardly he experiences himself as "nobody," but outwardly he plays the part of a giant. His natural dominance, usually expressed in his energetic and enthusiastic response to life, tends to drown out most of his fears and hesitations.

Role-playing provides these teen-agers with a fluid means for coping with the tension they experience between their need for self-expression and the social requirement to adjust. Extraverts are greatly concerned about the impression they make; they struggle to adapt, hoping to gain the acceptance of many, but this is not to say that they enjoy adapting. Quite the contrary, they would much rather do their own thing. This is why extravert adolescents like to be free to tune in and out of situations, to shift gears quickly, and to be at liberty to move. They thrive in environments that are fluid and accepting rather than fine-tuned and studied. Still, when it comes down to it, the applause of many is never completely satisfying: they hunger to be deeply and comprehensively understood.

These adolescents are intensely aware of their feelings and emotions; contrasting and conflicting emotions bombard them so powerfully that they can rise to the heights and sink to the depths in a matter of seconds. Extraverts are no strangers to loneliness and despair, but there are moments of ecstasy too—moments that they would give their whole life to hold onto, but which always elude their grasp.

The extravert teen-ager is aware that his inner life is dark and complicated, and he has a difficult time accepting the negative emotions that flare up so readily, so unexpectedly, and so frequently. The extravert realizes that he can't express them in every situation and that most people don't seem to have these problems. His inner life is so unpredictable that he has to anchor himself in concrete reality; so much is going on inside that he has to relate to people and situations just as they are. Because he sees aspects of his own inner experience mirrored in the many different kinds of people he is drawn to, he develops a tremendous capacity for empathy. Seeing others struggle with problems similar to his own also makes it easier for him to accept himself.

Nevertheless, the extravert adolescent can't always trust his natural flow of empathy all the way—especially when it comes to close relationships. It is important to be clear here: the extravert has many people whom he cares for very deeply. When I speak here of close relationship, I am referring to a comprehensive commitment like marriage. This kind of relationship often generates some anxiety because it is so reminiscent of early conflicts with the extravert's parents;

as an emotionally close relationship begins to develop, ambivalent feelings begin to flood his consciousness. When tension mounts, many of these extraverts take refuge in drugs and alcohol; others divorce sex from love and pursue it as an end in itself.

When an extravert adolescent does happen to let down all the barriers in one fell swoop, he can fall very deeply in love. But as his introverted desires for close relationship surface, they begin clashing with his strongly individualistic style of relating; that is why the virtue of temperance insists on moderation. The extravert needs a more gradual approach to close relationship so that there is enough time for his ambivalent feelings to clear.

Introvert Adolescent

Everyone over-identifies with his parents during infancy, but the introvert retains a residue of this over-identification, which continues to influence his relationship style throughout life. Because the introvert youngster buries so much of his own individuality and relies so heavily upon his parents for emotional support, over-identification constitutes a special danger for him, especially during the adolescent years. While identification is a conscious process involving people with somewhat similar experiences, over-identification is an unconscious process in which a person passively incorporates the thoughts and feelings of another person without relating them to his own experience. He swallows them whole, as it were, and allows them to influence him without consciously assimilating them.

Prior to adolescence, most introverts feel much like their parents about what really matters. They'll disagree and argue about unimportant issues, but deep down they depend more on their parents' experience than they do on their own. In contrast to extraverts, who must work hard in restraining the expression of their instincts and emotions, introverts have very little to curtail. However, when introverts enter their teens, they realize that they have to prepare themselves for adult life. As a result, they begin evaluating their own experiences and start making more decisions themselves.

Introvert adolescents are keenly aware of their need to move away from emotional dependence on their parents. Although the pull toward their parents

77

is strong and easily surrendered to, most introverts realize how unrealistic it is and struggle hard to overcome it. They try not to let their shyness get the better of them and concentrate on developing close relationships outside the family circle; those who strive to gain acceptance by "pleasing" instead of opening up and sharing themselves with others often end up feeling alone and empty inside. Introverts who fail to develop close relationships during adolescence are usually afraid of exploring their emerging thoughts and feelings with someone else because their identity is still so bound up with their parents; they haven't yet begun to discover what they think and how they feel as distinct from their parents.

Because introverts often fear that expressing their own individuality will threaten or endanger their close relationships, they tend to focus more on the needs of the ones they love than on their own. This tendency helps to distinguish them from introverted ambiverts, who, in spite of their natural reserve, have a strong sense of their own needs and recognize the importance of meeting them.

Although introvert adolescents are naturally reserved, they usually rest more comfortably within themselves when they have the security of a close relationship to rely on. When this security is threatened, storm clouds gather, and a feeling of sadness creeps over them. These adolescents yearn for an emotionally secure relationship more than anything else in the world. They try to approach a new relationship gradually because they know they have to "play it cool" to keep from getting hurt, but inside it's an all or nothing feeling. If introverts get sexually involved before marriage, they're apt to be motivated by a fear of losing someone special unless they make this concession. Most introverts feel more secure when they are going steady and can look forward to an early engagement; they realize that their emotional ties with their parents will eventually have to be transferred to a prospective marriage partner.

Ambivert Adolescent

Ambivert adolescents quickly discover that the way others respond to them depends to a great extent upon the way they respond to others. Extraverted ambiverts learn when it is to their advantage to give way to self-expression and when it isn't. Likewise, introverted ambiverts find that close relationships are more rewarding when they are sensitive to other people's rights. Such awareness increases self-confidence by giving ambiverts some measure of control over their environment; it also gives them a sense of security by making their life more predictable. Moreover, this awareness affects the way ambiverts think and feel about themselves. It's easier for them to be courteous if someone offends them because they know that being polite is to their advantage. Ambiverts aren't afraid to stand up for their rights, and they don't let people walk all over them, but they can and often do put up with unpleasant situations when they feel that it will serve their over-all interests. This is why ambiverts put so much time and energy into assessing people and situations.

Although extraverted ambiverts are more naturally tuned into self-expression, they also retain a healthy respect for values associated with close relationships. Similarly, although introverted ambiverts are more sensitive to close relationships, they also maintain a certain respect for values associated with self-expression. Both personality structures are rational and realistic, with a legitimate difference in emphasis. Both have a natural respect for the less dominant value even though they don't have a natural feeling for it; this respect is an integral part of their value system.

Although introverted ambiverts are very generous to those they love, they seldom give way to feelings and desires that might lead to emotional dependence. These adolescents rarely risk sharing personal feelings unless the atmosphere is just right and they are sure of complete acceptance. They value their privacy. Because they are much more comfortable listening, these teenagers usually depend on others to do most of the talking. They concentrate so much on the other person and are so eager to make the best possible response that they often seem to be more of an observer than a real participant in a relationship. Sometimes they feel that they give more than they receive because their friends aren't tuned into their unexpressed feelings.

Extraverted ambiverts like people with very diverse interests. Although adolescents often feel that their need for self-expression is cramped by social structures and conventions, they are in a double bind because their early identity is so bound up with their social role and public image; they also want to achieve success and gain the respect of the broader community. These teenagers usually resolve this conflict by restricting their more spontaneous forms of self-expression to less conventional settings.

79

All ambiverts are caught in the tension between two conflicting desires. For introverted ambiverts, the desire to keep their feelings to themselves conflicts with their desire for close relationship. For extraverted ambiverts, the desire to achieve a respected place in society conflicts with their desire for greater freedom of self-expression. Both strive to free themselves from an undue concern for what others may think.

Ambivert adolescents take initiative while still sticking closely to the social structures that ground them. When they experiment and test the boundaries of these structures, their own experience teaches them how to be comfortably self-directing. Ambivert adolescents usually try to look on the bright side of a situation and make up their minds to put up with whatever comes along with it, but when the negative elements begin to outweigh the positive, they make plans to move on.

Ambivert teen-agers usually identify with the existing norms for adolescence, but even when falling in love, they rarely lose sight of the over-all picture. The values of education, career, financial security, and social status — which are so much a part of the society with which they identify — are deeply entrenched. All these different aspects of life are woven together into a single fabric. They entered into their consciousness as children and seem "right" simply because they have become so much a part of them. This awareness grounds them in a strong sense of who they are and what they want.

In contrast to the instinctual and emotional inhibitions of introvert children and the heightened instinctual and emotional reactions of extravert children, ambivert children usually maintain a fairly even keel. Nevertheless, some ambivert teen-agers avoid dealing with the interpersonal challenges of adolescence by concentrating all their energy on developing practical skills. (This is especially tempting in a technologically advanced society like ours, which places so much emphasis on "getting ahead.") As a result, perfectly good natural tendencies frequently turn into drives that are locked in battle with equally strong controls — controls that are reinforced by the ambivert's strong identification with society.

IV

LOVE: ITS EVOLUTION

WHEN I SAY that the extravert's first phase of development is characterized by self-expression and the introvert's by close relationship, I don't mean to infer that self-expression and close relationship reach maturity during the first phase of development. On the contrary, self-expression in the extravert is marred by an exaggerated sense of his own individuality, which results in a kind of self-centeredness that is very difficult for him to overcome — or even to detect. Self-expression is experienced by the extravert as an exuberant celebration of who he is; it contains the essence of his individuality. Letting go of self-expression would mean fading into oblivion and losing an essential hold on who he is. The positive and negative threads of self-expression are all woven together into a single piece of cloth. When even a single thread is pulled, he panics. The mere thought of inhibiting his natural flow of energy terrifies him, for this flow *is* himself. Touching the fragile core of one's identity is very delicate business.

The same holds true of the introvert in regard to close relationship. During the first phase of development, close relationship is usually hampered by a kind of possessiveness that tends to shut out the rest of the world. Introverts have a hard time recognizing this flaw because their apparently altruistic desire for close relationship is so intimately tied up with their own needs. But it is this very sensitivity that leads the introvert to a discovery of who he is. Still, the fact remains that the more an introvert strives to increase his sensitivity to those he loves, the more persistently the weeds of possessiveness threaten to choke out the good of the relationship. But to uproot one would be to uproot the other; both have to grow together until the harvest. That is how intricately the positive and negative aspects of close relationship are intertwined. It's no wonder that introverts experience their underpinnings being pulled out from under them when

81

OUTER RINGS

INTROVERT

EXTRAVERT

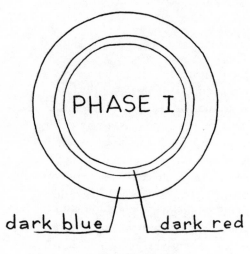

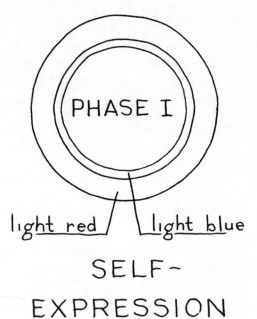

dark blue / dark red

light red / light blue

CLOSE
RELATIONSHIP

SELF~
EXPRESSION

Figure 22

a close relationship is threatened. The fragile core of their identity is shaken at its roots.

From everything that has been said so far, it should be clear that introverts aren't any closer to *mature* close relationships than extraverts are to *mature* self-expression. It should also be obvious that any movement from one phase of growth to another is difficult and should never be forced. These transitions must follow their own natural course of growth, but this isn't to say that growth can't be retarded or even stunted when its momentum is resisted.

Figure 22 represents somewhat typical dynamics that occur between introverts and extraverts during their first phase of development. The two outer rings representing this phase are abstracted from the psychic energy circles (see figures 14 and 16, pages 46 and 50). These "first phase" dynamics are most dramatically illustrated by the experience of falling in love because love is a peak experience that helps people to prepare for a move from one phase of growth to another.

In the description that follows, a female introvert and a male extravert fall in love. The magnetism of the introvert/extravert dynamics coupled with the male/female attraction intensifies them, but the female is just as likely to be an extravert, and the male an introvert. In our story, the experience of falling in love goes something like this:

An introvert is attracted to a naturally outgoing extravert who asks her for a date. She is happy to have such an exciting and stimulating young man ask her out, and she wants to know everything about him; it's hard for her to comprehend how any one person can be involved in so many different things. Taking a personal interest in everything he does opens up many new dimensions of her life, and she is delighted to have found someone who can share himself in such a lively way. The introvert feels herself expanding in many different directions and considers herself privileged to be so personally involved in every aspect of her friend's life. Stepping out *with* the extravert enables her to enjoy the excitement of meeting many new and interesting people — something she wouldn't be inclined to do if she were on her own.

The extravert is also pleased to have such a charming and sensitive companion who is interested in everything about him and eager to help him in any way she can. What more could he ask for? It's obvious how devoted she is to him. Such an ideal atmosphere is conducive for taking emotional risks; gradually a whole new world opens up for him, in which he is no longer lonely, and he is amazed to discover how much he has been missing.

Falling in love makes it possible for both of them to expand their fragile inner core painlessly and without effort; as new horizons open up, they go beyond their previous limitations—even without realizing it.

The introvert is like an empty vessel that the extravert delights in filling with himself—his vitality, his enthusiasm, his hopes, and his dreams—and he enjoys basking in the warmth and tenderness of the introvert's unconditional love. The dark and negative feelings that used to flare up so unexpectedly begin to diminish as he learns to trust more deeply and begins to rest in the peaceful serenity of the introvert's love. The extravert is re-experiencing what it's like to become emotionally interdependent—something he hasn't experienced since very early childhood.

Sometime during the second phase of their relationship (see figure 23, over), the introvert begins to feel a little uneasy about the extravert. She is extremely sensitive, touchy, and even tearful, but she can't quite put her finger on what's really bothering her, so she brushes these unpleasant and disturbing feelings away. Still, the feelings return, and the introvert becomes moody; no matter how hard she tries, nothing seems to work. The introvert knows there is no "objective" reason for feeling the way she does; nothing has changed, and everything is the same as usual. Yet her feelings persist.

When the extravert asks her what's wrong, she is at a loss for words. She craves his affection more than ever and is grateful for his concern, but she really doesn't know what is the matter with her, and so she ends up assuring him that everything is okay.

However, everything isn't okay. Gradually, traces of more disturbing feelings begin to surface, and the introvert finds herself irritable and resentful about little things. These feelings distress her. She doesn't like to think of herself this way, so she tries to hide how she is feeling—even from herself.

Once again, the extravert tries to draw her out, and once more, she tries to reassure him that nothing is wrong, but the extravert is not so easily convinced

MIDDLE RINGS

INTROVERT   EXTRAVERT

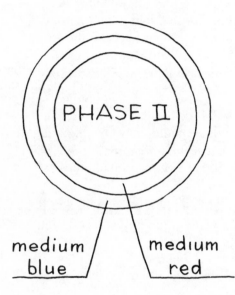
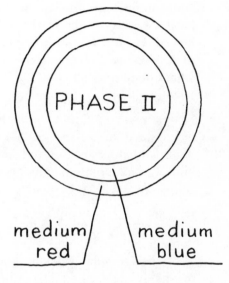

Figure 23

this time. He can see she's not herself, and he picks up a trace of resentment in her voice, even when she is trying to convince him that everything is fine.

Gradually, barely perceptible movements of anger begin stirring within her and they suddenly erupt into volcanic proportions as she lashes out at the extravert about a mere nothing. It's hard to say which of them is the more surprised and dismayed; both are caught completely off guard.

After apologizing, the introvert quickly resorts to more adaptive behavior while protesting loudly and profusely that she didn't mean it, but no matter how hard she tries to convince him that nothing is wrong, the extravert is not convinced. He knows that something *is* wrong, and he is sure that it has something to do with *him*. Nothing can dissuade him — this time he is determined to find out what's bothering her.

The introvert is embarrassed and stumbles all over herself trying to regain her composure. She keeps telling herself that she shouldn't be feeling this way — she didn't intend for this to happen. But her feelings erupted in spite of herself. She is ashamed and upset because she didn't live up to her image of herself as a kind and loving person.

The extravert repeats his question, a bit impatiently this time; she can tell he won't take no for an answer. Finally, with tears streaming down her cheeks and choking back her sobs, she exclaims, "You're so selfish!"

He is completely taken aback, but is eager to hear the worst. "What do you mean?" he insists.

"We always do everything *your* way," she blurts out. "You never do anything *I* want. It's always what *you* want. It's all so one-sided!"

"What can she possibly mean!" the extravert mutters under his breath as he walks over to the window. He is shocked; he never gave as much to anyone as he has given to her. It hasn't always been easy for him to trust and share so much of himself. He had put everything he could into the relationship. Anger begins to surge within him, but beneath the anger is a wound too raw to touch: he is deeply hurt. The extravert knows better than to express himself when he is angry, for he has learned from long, hard experience how disastrous rashness can be. He needs time to reflect prudently on what she said and temper his reaction to it so that he can make a decision that is just and fair for both of them. As

86

he backs away from the window, he turns to her and says, "We'll talk about this later." Then he slips quickly out of the room.

The introvert is stunned and panic-stricken — the extravert is drawing back from her when she needs him most. She feels as if everything is lost, that nothing will ever be the same again. Her whole world is shattered. Running after him, she flings her arms around him and sobs, "Can't we make up first?"

"No, I need time to myself," he replies as he gently but firmly releases himself from her embrace.

She is angry and deeply humiliated, but this time she is glad for her anger — glad for the courage it gives her to be less dependent. Deep down she knows she needs that.

Meanwhile the extravert is struggling with his own feelings; he felt stifled and trapped in her arms. The more she pleaded and clung to him, the angrier he got; being so much his own person, he had expected her to have more respect for herself than to stoop to something like this. "She is not as predictable as I thought — perhaps I went too far by placing so much trust in her," he mused.

One afternoon, a week later, he asks her, "What is it that you want to do? You said I never do what you like. What do you like to do?"

His companion stops short. She isn't prepared for the question, but she is relieved to be really talking again after a week of polite chitchat. In spite of his apparently cautious distance, she detects a note of earnestness in his voice, and she can tell from the way he is looking at her that he is serious. The introvert pauses for a moment, searching for a response that doesn't come. Finally, with tears beginning to well up in her eyes, she looks at him and says, "I really don't know. . . ."

And she really didn't! The introvert fell deeply in love with him largely because he embodied so many of her own buried feelings and desires that are now struggling to emerge *in herself*. When they do, there will be a much better equilibrium in the relationship, but until then, she will have to work hard at tempering her excessive desires and respecting her partner's need for distance.

During the second phase of the relationship, the natural flow of energy is seeking to find its way into broader channels. Falling in love made it all possible, but now the honeymoon is over. This is the time of life when most women become more active and start doing more things on their own. Men undergo various changes too; they sometimes change jobs or get additional education. Both partners need more independence in order to maintain a good equilibrium while working out their relationship. There are, of course, those who ignore their relationship problems and invest *all* their energy outside the home. When this happens, the relationship is likely to deteriorate.

Realistically, such a relationship needs a strong commitment to carry it through this difficult period. Never before has the introvert experienced so many changeable and conflicting emotions—emotions that are intricately bound up with a need to come more into her own, and which contain the basic ingredients she needs for a deeper grounding in herself. The introvert needs to unravel the threads of her identity as distinct from that of her partner in order to free herself from the excessive dependence that she previously viewed as love. Only by identifying her own feelings and desires, while at the same time respecting those of her partner, will she be able to right the balance of over-dependence by developing a healthy measure of independence.

Emotional honesty is especially difficult for introverts, not only because it interferes with their self-image but also because it disturbs the good feelings on which they depend so heavily in close relationships. As a result, many introverts try to manipulate and control their partners in subtle and indirect ways, and once such a pattern is established, it's very hard to break.

In figure 23, page 85, the medium blue and red rings of equal width represent the introvert's need to establish a new emotional equilibrium by accepting and owning that part of herself that is separate and distinct from her partner. Once she has achieved this independence, it will be easier for her to be true to herself and to her partner.

In the same figure, the medium red and blue rings of equal width represent the extravert's need to establish a new equilibrium by putting self-expression at the service of close relationship as he learns how to be true to his partner as well as to himself.

Meanwhile, the extravert's task is every bit as challenging as the introvert's. Falling in love resurrected his buried desires for close relationship, and now he has to struggle with the pain of disillusionment, resentment, and anger. His days of basking in the sunshine of the introvert's idolatrous, selfless, and untiring devotion are over; now he has to concentrate on justice in the relationship. He does his best to give due consideration to her wishes, even when she isn't immediately aware of her feelings and desires, and he waits for her response so that they can collaborate in decision making. Although he sincerely tries to understand her, he really can't fathom the differences between them — sometimes it seems like a bottomless abyss.

More often than not, he feels as if he's just playing a role to ease the situation for her, but deep down, he knows it's more than that. He too is struggling with his own unrealistic expectations of close relationship arising out of early childhood conflicts and resulting in an exaggerated sense of his own individuality. Every extravert knows how to enjoy himself, and it's natural for him to be the center of attention. Stepping back and allowing someone else to take center stage is difficult even under the best of circumstances, but especially when he is hurting. Accepting the introvert "as she is" and focusing on her needs — needs he doesn't even understand — goes against the grain. "Why," he asks himself, "did I allow myself to become emotionally interdependent with such an unpredictable person?" Now that these feelings are awakened, there's no turning back!

Or is there?

The extravert feels as if the fragile and delicate shoot of his new-found ability to entrust himself deeply to another person is in danger of withering. It's natural for the extravert to attract others by expressing his own individuality, but there comes a time when an extravert is no longer completely satisfied by the applause of many. He knows he has another side that others don't see, and he sometimes fears it will never be understood — even by himself. This introverted side, representing his less conscious needs for emotional intimacy, is in danger of drying up if he does not create the opportunity for working through close relationships. The extravert has the opportunity of re-establishing a new equilibrium between self-expression and close relationship. Will he recognize it and accept it as a gift?

It could go either way; everything is going against the natural grain in both of them. The ecstacy of falling in love launched them all unaware into the deeper water of the second phase of development, and now the rough waves of disillusionment are threatening the relationship. Will the extravert resist the momentum of growth and swing back to the shallow waters of the previous phase?

At this point, everything depends on the moral virtues; each personality type has a natural aptitude for certain aspects of the virtues. In childhood each was encouraged to build on his natural tendencies, as long as certain extremes were avoided. However, something more is required in the second phase of development.

Both are being asked to build on the experience of falling in love, and that means acquiring some virtues that don't come *naturally*. After having successfully developed the virtues aligned with her natural tendencies, the introvert clearly reached an impasse that hampered her further development in virtue. Because she was not sufficiently aware of her own feelings, desires, and even needs, she was having difficulty expressing herself appropriately. Similarly, although the extravert tried to be virtuous by inhibiting self-expression, he obviously had little natural sensitivity to the introvert's needs or to close relationship. Both need to develop the virtues of prudence, justice, temperance, and fortitude in a whole new dimension and in a very different way. Now that the introvert is struggling with self-expression and the extravert with close relationship, they will be concentrating on different aspects of virtue. The independence that characterizes the second phase of growth evolves from the development of these new virtues.

Phase three (see figure 24) begins when the tension between self-expression and close relationship begins to give way to a more authentic experience of oneself in relation to one's partner. This is when the struggle to develop the virtues of prudence, justice, fortitude, and temperance in the previous two phases begins to pay off. The desire for close relationship now holds such a strong attraction for the extravert that it begins to merge with his natural tendency for self-expression. Similarly, the desire for self-expression attracts the introvert to such an extent that it begins to merge with her natural desire for close relationship.

Perhaps the most significant development is the discovery of a whole new rhythm between self-expression and close relationship for both introvert and extravert as their natural tendencies are diverted into broader channels that excite and energize them. The introvert is more spontaneous because she is no longer afraid of expressing herself inappropriately. In figure 24 the light blue ring

90

INNER RINGS

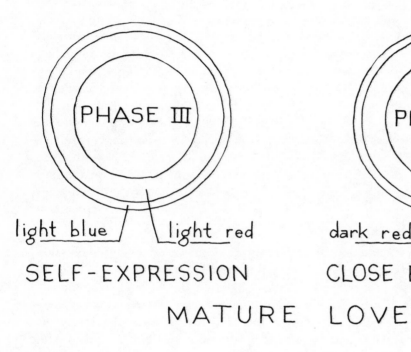
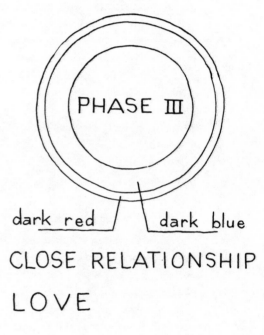

INTROVERT

EXTRAVERT

PHASE III

PHASE III

light blue / light red

dark red / dark blue

SELF-EXPRESSION

CLOSE RELATIONSHIP

MATURE LOVE

Figure 24

represents the ease with which the introvert is able to accept the limitations of close relationship; the light red ring represents the lighthearted and supple expansiveness of her self-expression. Likewise, the extravert is more intimate and no longer afraid to reveal his own vulnerability in close relationship. In the same figure, the dark red ring represents the emotional intensity that draws the extravert toward deeper intimacy; the dark blue ring represents the depth at which the extravert absorbs the different aspects of close relationship. As introvert and extravert approach mature love, they begin reaping the fruits of the virtues that they sowed in the struggles of the previous phases.

V

PERSONALITY DEVELOPMENT

Ambivert Development

The origin of personality type can be traced all the way back to the womb and early infancy when the child is still unable to distinguish between himself and his mother. Everyone shares this common heritage and carries within himself the effect of its early imprint. But it is more intensely and immediately experienced by the child as he emerges from the subterranean world of the womb; an infant is totally at the mercy of his environment.

All children are tossed like a ball between a backward pull to the womb and a forward pull to grow up. But the conflict seems to reach a greater degree of intensity in extraverts and introverts. When the tension between these two conflicting drives peaks, one drive gains such ascendancy that it all but obliterates the other. This is when clear patterns of introverted and extraverted behavior begin to emerge.

It is somewhat different for ambiverts. Although introverted ambiverts usually display a marked preference for close relationships and extraverted ambiverts for self-expression, it soon becomes clear that their energy is really being invested in their own developing independence. This independence becomes rooted in their body in and through the development of practical skills, which create a natural bridge to the outside world. These skills not only provide ambiverts with many opportunities for self-expression but also lend themselves to fostering close relationships. This early emphasis on independence shortens the length of time that ambiverts are plagued by the conflict between the backward pull to the womb and the forward pull to grow up. Their natural excitement over

93

all that they are learning to do energizes them. Without their even realizing it, the early conflict is resolved, and they are well on their way to a successful latency.

Latency is the period of time between seven and twelve when the instinctual and emotional spontaneity of the preceding years declines dramatically. It normally coincides with the child's entrance into school when he begins to learn the rudiments of reading, writing, and arithmetic—subjects that are usually too dry to arouse the interest of a younger child. Latency provides the opportunity for all children to establish the rational structure they need to offset the impact of early instincts and emotions, and school provides them with the education they need to make sense of the world in which they live. The ambivert's instinctual flow of energy is so naturally invested in the experience of latency that it can be considered an "ambivert" phase that all children pass through, but in which only the ambivert's identity is rooted. Latency insulates most children—at least to some extent—from the excesses of earlier instincts and emotions; it normally offers them a respite before early conflicts crop up again in a new disguise during adolescence.

The ambivert's experience of adolescence is strongly influenced by his emphasis on independence and the development of practical skills that helped to establish a firm personality structure during latency. But this structure is not so airtight that it cannot be altered as some interests deepen and others decline to make room for new ones at the beginning of adolescence. Although the ambivert's identity remains rooted in latency, it's base broadens as instincts and emotions begin to reawaken, and the adolescent begins questioning certain aspects of established social structures that he formerly accepted at face value. Recognizing the limitations of society helps him to differentiate between his own principles and the norms of society.

While their minds are busy examining their individual relationship to society, ambiverts' hearts are engaged in an emotional tug-of-war between family and peer relationships. As the sap begins to rise in the springtime of adolescence, their bodies also begin changing and sexual instincts start clamoring for an expression that has to be tempered. Moreover, all these changes are occurring within the parameters of their fine-tuned, sensory-perceptual personality organization.

94

As previously stated, ambivert children formerly resolved their conflict between the backward pull to the womb and the forward pull to grow up through the development of practical skills. But what is adequate for one stage of growth is seldom adequate for another. During adolescence, earlier instincts and emotions re-emerge in new forms and begin seeping through the foundations that were laid during latency as they impatiently insist on integration.

Once again the ambivert is faced with the problem of conflicting desires. Part of him would like to ignore the changes that are now taking place — preferring to stick with the simple solutions that worked for him so well during latency; another part of him would like to pull out all the stops — going all the way with the rising sap of sexual instincts and forget everything else. Ordinarily too much of the ambivert's identity is tied up with society for him to take such an extreme all-or-nothing approach. Most ambiverts want to have their cake and eat it too, and society provides a number of possible options. However, the virtue of temperance demands much more than making a satisfactory adjustment to society, where compromise on one side is usually compensated for by satisfaction on the other. Temperance helps the ambivert to integrate his sexual instincts and the emotions that accompany them into the over-all structure of his personality; it encourages him to expand the fine-tuned, sensory-perceptual foundation of his personality that was laid down during latency and to make room for the new growth that is occurring during adolescence.

Ambiverts are naturally independent and like to be in control of their lives, but the need for integration underlies the problem of control. Unless instincts and emotions that surface during adolescence find their rightful place within the over-all structure of the personality, control becomes much more difficult. If this integration is not achieved, sexual instincts begin warring and competing with the work-related skills that were laid down during latency.

Temperance insists that all the natural tendencies work harmoniously together by curbing the excess of any one tendency struggling to gain ascendancy over the others. This virtue won't allow one tendency to gain such prominence that it threatens to dominate — or even obliterate — another. Temperance ensures that the different parts of the personality work together for the benefit of the whole; it leads to wholeness by helping us to achieve integration in our lives.

95

Introvert Development

The introvert child's pull back to the womb gains a strong ascendancy over his forward pull to grow up. This is not to say that the introvert doesn't grow up—only that his vital life energy is very much bound up with his parents. Just as the ambivert gains a sense of security by developing practical skills, the introvert gains a sense of security by relying on the parental bond. Although the introvert also develops practical skills, which contribute to his growth as an autonomous and independent person, the parental bond is really what motivates him and supplies the emotional energy he needs for these tasks.

Parental ties are so strong that they provide the structural foundation of the personality. Introverts often live more through their parents than through themselves; such an over-identification excludes the expression of individual differences and creates a void that is filled with idealistic fantasies—fantasies that stand in sharp contrast to the realities that confront these children when they start school. Yet these fantasies represent some of their deepest feelings and desires and are intimately bound up with their most fundamental experience of who they are. That is why introvert children sometimes feel different until they develop close relationships with other introverts. Such relationships help to siphon off some of the excess emotions bound up with their parents, and this goes a long way toward helping introverts to make a successful transition between home and school.

During latency the introvert child tends to view his teacher as a kind of second mother—and "pleasing" in this particular situation usually means being very conscientious about school work. The threads of an introvert child's achievement motivation are almost always woven into the warp of his emotional attachment to parents. Some introverts concentrate so hard on pleasing that grades—the yardstick that is normally used to measure progress—become an end in themselves. If a child becomes too preoccupied with obtaining good grades, this sometimes snuffs out the spark of genuine interest and prevents it from developing.

The introvert child's experience of latency is very different from that of the ambivert child. His creativity is almost always subject to a longer incubation period, during which much is unconsciously absorbed into the deeper recesses of the personality. Although the length of this time period varies, it seems to have

96

some bearing upon the degree of creativity released once the introvert awakens to his own individuality. He typically begins the search for his individuality during adolescence and usually takes some concrete steps in that direction before it is over. Much depends on how long the introvert spends "incubating" before his individuality begins asserting itself; this is almost certainly related to the degree of introversion.

Most introvert adolescents realize that too much of their identity is bound up with that of their parents, but they have very different ways of dealing with the problem. Some introverts differentiate themselves intellectually by disagreeing with their parents' ideas long before they separate themselves emotionally; intellectual development seems to permit some of their individuality to emerge while keeping the underlying emotional bond intact. Still others seem to walk a tightrope by maintaining a very delicate and precarious emotional balance between an overly dependent relationship and one that leaves room for their individual growth. In spite of the contrast between these different approaches, all introverts rely on ideas to help differentiate themselves from their parents; the introverts' individuality emerges as they begin to *reflect* more on their own experience. This accounts for their characteristically reserved and reflective manner that distinguishes their relationship style from that of the extravert.

Adolescence provides the opportunity for a replay of the original experience between parent and child under very different circumstances and at a much higher level of maturity. As the instinctual and emotional energies that have been hibernating during latency are released, introverts strive to channel them away from their parents and toward their peers, relying heavily upon parental attitudes to support them in this. The parents who refuse to "let go" make it more difficult for these adolescents.

The experience of falling in love challenges the introvert to take the first step in overcoming the effects of early childhood conditioning, but even under the best of circumstances, he has to be careful not to repeat the same old patterns. Viewing himself as an extension of the one he loves brings him dangerously close to obliterating a good portion of his own emerging individuality and prevents him from seeing the other person as he or she really is. This danger is probably the most fundamental reason for the introvert's characteristic need to turn inward and reflect — to avoid over-identifying; *it is the fear of obliterating his own individuality through over-identification that sometimes goes so far as to inhibit the desire*

97

for close relationship entirely. In order to "temper" his natural tendency for over-identification, the introvert must concentrate more on being true to himself and to his own needs than on pleasing or placating others.

Extravert Development

Although the extravert's genetic make-up almost certainly predisposes him to precocious instinctual and emotional development, his mother's physical and psychological condition during pregnancy also has an effect on him. Once the child is born, much depends on the quality of his interaction with the environment. This complex interplay of contributing circumstances makes it difficult to pinpoint precisely what determines personality type. But one thing is sure: parents can do much to encourage the constructive aspects of the child's natural tendencies.

At a certain point in the child's development, the extravert experiences a sharp contrast between close relationship and self-expression. Although self-expression wins out, it is simply an outward expression of the extravert's *heightened* instinctual and emotional awareness, and this intensity helps to distinguish him from the extraverted ambivert. But why does the extravert's premature desire to grow up overpower his need for a longer period of emotional dependence?

The extravert child has an uncanny ability to pick up emotional tension in the environment; when his parents are upset, he feels it. He is highly susceptible to an emotionally charged environment and automatically reacts to it. This interferes with his ability to depend upon his parents for emotional security as much as he would like. Whereas the introvert child attempts to block out emotional stimuli and manipulates the parental bond on which he relies so heavily, the extravert relies on his own instinctual and emotional reactions to whatever is disturbing him. Each protects himself in a different way. The introvert child turns inward and tries to cope by unconsciously manipulating his parents; the extravert child turns outward and tries to cope by relying on his own resources—which sometimes fall short.

Many different circumstances can reinforce this premature self-reliance. For example, some parents are so charmed by the extravert child's instinctual

98

and emotional spontaneity that they spoil him by indulging his every whim. However, once the "cute" stage passes and a new baby arrives, the pattern changes quite dramatically: the child feels cast aside like an old toy that has been replaced by a bright, shining new one. His craving for affection clamors for gratification, and he feels let down because he now equates love with the instinctual and emotional high he had come to depend on. Too young to recognize the difference between being loved and being spoiled, he feels deprived of something that is rightfully his. As frustration mounts, he begins testing his parents — hoping they will change — but eventually comes to realize that he has to accept the situation the way it is. This acceptance provides the extravert with the security of realistic boundaries he can count on, but it doesn't make up for the deprivation he experiences.

Most extraverts resolve this dilemma by trying to grow up as quickly as possible; they are eager to come into their own. Taking care of younger children and assuming responsiblity for household chores gives them more status and makes them feel grown up. But at the same time, they also begin seeking instinctual and emotional gratification outside the family circle. This results in a dramatic shift in the way their psychic energy is channeled. Once extraverts try their wings, there is no stopping them. They try coping with problems well beyond their years and eventually become quite adept at dealing with the unexpected. Extravert children frequently assume more than their fair share of burdens and often undertake more than they are capable of. This is how they come to rely so much on an exaggerated sense of their own individuality.

When the extravert starts school, he soons discovers that it's not all fun and games. He is alert and quick to catch on to whatever interests him, but it's hard for him to adjust to a systematic approach to learning. The extravert has so much instinctual energy that it is difficult for him to concentrate on something that doesn't hold his interest. When he is bored, instinctual impulses and reactions rush in to fill the void. It isn't that the extravert doesn't want to learn — it's just that he is more interested in learning through experience, and any other approach is apt to have a straitjacket effect on him.

During latency, most extraverts test their teachers just as they did their parents; they need to know how much they can get away with. Extravert children usually go overboard by clowning around and showing off — until adults help them to establish a rhythm between impulse and control by setting limits. But eventually their craving for pleasure and their need for testing are transformed into a desire to reach out even more broadly. Extraverts want to explore the world and its pleasures, but they also know the world will impose limits on them. Sooner or later, most extraverts reach a point where they don't want to keep learning the hard way, so they try to obtain as much information as they can about the world and the way it functions. This knowledge helps them to bridge the gap between their need for self-expression and the social pressure to conform — something that most extraverts wrestle with for a long time.

Some extraverts try to resolve their conflict between an exaggerated sense of their own individuality and a desire for social status by seeking a position of authority where they can operate with a minimum of outside control. Being their own boss helps to reduce this tension by allowing some of their individuality to merge with their position. For some extraverts, however, their individuality becomes synonymous with the exercise of authority, and they can no longer distinguish between a legitimate and illegitimate use of authority. Needless to say, this is an unhealthy and destructive way of resolving the conflict.

During adolescence, the extravert's more recessive desire for close relationship begins to surface and mingles with his more dominant desire for self-expression, which has already gained a foothold in his personality. This generates strong emotional reactions that have their roots in early childhood experiences. Some extraverts seem to be more influenced by pleasant memories; others, by painful ones. But either way, extravert adolescents usually try to avoid complex emotional entanglements by concentrating on enjoying carefree, pleasurable relationships with persons of the opposite sex. Many extravert adolescents are very open about themselves, and their friends frequently mistake this for real intimacy. However, extravert adolescents often fear deep emotional intimacy because it presses them to find a new resolution for their earlier conflict between close relationship and self-expression. This is, of course, just what the virtues of temperance and fortitude challenge them to do.

VI

JACOB AND ESAU:
INTROVERT AND EXTRAVERT

Now THAT you have some idea of what introversion and extraversion are about, I'd like to interpret the story of Jacob and Esau so that you can see the introvert and extravert personality dynamics at work in a real-life situation. The theme of the story — found in Genesis, the first book of the Old Testament — relates to the rivalry between twin brothers: Jacob the introvert, and Esau, the extravert. Highlighting the contrasting dynamics of their personality types reveals the different paths that introverts and extraverts take in their psychological and moral development. Soon you may find yourself feeling more sympathy for one brother than the other — and perhaps that will tell you something about yourself.

This story, which has been told and retold in countless variations down through the ages, demonstrates the existence of introvert and extravert personality types as early as 1500 B.C. Recognizing the universal nature of introverted and extraverted dynamics enables us to get beyond a sense of isolation and fear born of an overly personal or clinical approach to individual and interpersonal problems and helps us to view them in a broader perspective as part of the human condition. This frees us from a self-conscious feeling of shame, enabling us to get more deeply in touch with our inner experience — thereby increasing our capacity for creative self-awareness, which fosters psychological and moral growth.

The scriptural narrative reveals that the twins' parents, Isaac and Rebekah, waited twenty years before God answered their prayers for children. But no sooner did Rebekah become pregnant than the trouble began. The twins jostled each other so much while still in her womb that Rebekah became despondent — even to the point where she was beginning to wish that she had never become pregnant. Rebekah probably had something of a mother's intuition of even more trouble ahead when she consulted the Lord; He responded:

> "There are two nations in your womb,
> your issue will be two rival peoples.
> One nation shall have mastery of the other,
> and the elder shall serve the younger."
> (Gen. 25:23)

Rebekah was somewhat relieved, for her premonition had been confirmed —at least she knew she wasn't imagining things. There had been some reason for her depression, and now she had cause for optimism as well—her children were destined for greatness!

When Rebekah's time to deliver arrived, Esau was the first to appear; his brother followed, gripping Esau's heel. Almost as soon as the twins were born, the parents seemed to sense that Jacob was going to have a harder time holding his own, so they called him "Jacob," which is sometimes translated as "may God protect."

> When the boys grew up, Esau became a skilled hunter,
> a man of the open country. . . .
> (Gen. 25:27)

Here is an important clue to Esau's personality. The extravert needs wide, open spaces and cannot bear to be fenced in; he doesn't like anyone hovering over him and needs to strike out on his own.

> ". . . . Jacob on the other hand was a quiet man, staying
> at home among the tents."
> (Gen. 25:27)

For Jacob had the natural reserve of the introvert who prefers to conserve his energy by narrowing his focus and turning inward.

Parents of children with different personality types usually have their favorites—and Isaac and Rebekah were no exception. Isaac thrilled to Esau's tales of adventure as he returned from the hunt, elated and full of excitement, so full of courage and bravado. But it was Jacob's sensitivity to others, his quiet

102

reserve, and his serious, reflective manner that appealed to Rebekah and drew her toward him.

The twins also had strong reactions toward one another, for it was just as natural for Esau to see Jacob's underdeveloped extraverted side as it was for Jacob to see Esau's underdeveloped introverted side. From Esau's point of view, Jacob was a "mama's boy," always tied to Rebekah's apron strings. Why wasn't Jacob more virile, more rough and ready? Why wasn't he out there doing something? From Jacob's point of view, Esau was not only trying, but also very tiring. Esau was forever talking about himself and his doings, and he always seemed to have the knack of getting the whole world to revolve around him — without even trying! The outside world was the only world that he appreciated; he knew nothing of Jacob's inner world. But it was Esau's condescending attitude that caused Jacob the deepest pain, and because of it, he had quite a struggle remaining true to himself.

Once when Jacob was engaged in the unexciting task of making a soup, Esau returned from the hunt, full of vigor and eager to share his tales of high adventure. How many times this identical situation must have occurred before! But lately it had really begun to get on Jacob's nerves; he was getting fed up with Esau always taking him for granted. Jacob was no longer interested in Esau's breathtaking episodes.

> Esau said to Jacob, "Let me eat the red soup, that
> red soup there; I am exhausted". . . .
> (Gen. 25:30-32)

Notice Esau's brisk, unappreciative manner. He expected Jacob to respond in his usual way, but this time it was different. Jacob had *had* it.

> Jacob said, "First sell me your birthright, then."
> (Gen. 25:30-32)

Esau was shocked: Jacob couldn't be serious!

> Esau said, "Here I am at death's door; what use will my
> birthright be to me?"
> (Gen. 25:30-32)

But Jacob persisted and would be satisfied with nothing less than an oath, so Esau sold his birthright to him under oath.

103

Esau's birthright meant little to him. When the present moment failed to hold him, Esau was on to something else; he wanted to enjoy the here and now and had no inclination to delay present gratification for the sake of future gain.

With Jacob it was just the opposite. He loved to reflect and ponder — savoring every experience, and repeatedly bringing it back to mind like a cow chewing its cud. Jacob wasn't comfortable jumping right into something without thinking it through beforehand; he felt the need to sort things out.

Like many young introverts, Jacob tended to confuse love with being a "yes man," and he was just beginning to figure out the difference. Now he had acted with conviction in a very important matter; asserting himself with Esau by demanding his birthright was a big step forward — albeit an exaggerated one.

Time passed. Isaac's health began to fail, and his eyesight was growing dim. The time for Isaac to bestow his blessing on his eldest son was drawing near. One day Rebekah overheard Isaac ask Esau to bring him some game from the hunt and prepare an appetizing dish so that he could give Esau his special blessing before he died. Recalling what God had revealed to her about her older son serving the younger, Rebekah quickly called Jacob to her and instructed him to take Esau's place. She prepared an appetizing dish such as Isaac liked; then she gave Esau's best clothes for Jacob to wear, and covered his smooth hands and neck with goat skins, so that if Isaac should touch Jacob, he would think him Esau, whose hands and body were hairy.

Instead of assuming responsibility for his own actions, Jacob — like many young introverts — relied more on his mother's conscience than on his own. Because his over-identification with Rebekah led him astray, he was able to rationalize his deception without feeling guilty. Moreover, his mother certainly didn't help matters by assuring him that if anything went wrong, she would accept the blame.

In relying on Rebekah's assurances, Jacob mistook rashness for courage and approached his father. Psychologically speaking, the naturally shy and reserved Jacob was not only pretending to play the part of his brother, Esau, but was also asserting — both inwardly and outwardly — that he was like Esau. Instead of being true to himself and his own introversion, he was attempting to encounter his father with the confidence and self-assurance of an extravert.

In the ensuing dialogue between Jacob and his father, Isaac repeatedly asked Jacob if he was really Esau, and Jacob persisted in claiming that he was. Finally, having drawn Jacob close to him, Isaac was convinced and blessed him saying:

> "Yes, the smell of my son
> is like the smell of a fertile field
> blessed by Yahweh.
> May God give you
> dew from heaven,
> and the richness of the earth,
> abundance of grain and wine!
> May nations serve you
> and peoples bow down before you!
> Be master of your brothers;
> may the sons of your mother bow down before you!
> Cursed be he who curses you;
> blessed be he who blesses you!"
>
> (Gen. 27:28-29)

Jacob was very much aware of the promise God had made to Rebekah—that Esau, the older son, would serve the younger. Jacob would never have undertaken this difficult dialogue with his father without Rebekah's assurance that this is what God had intended. It seems likely that Jacob acted in good faith in following Rebekah's instructions, but he also had his own motives for acting as he did.

It seems that Jacob had recognized his jealousy toward his older brother ever since the day he demanded Esau's birthright; prior to that, he had simply served his brother without question. Now that he was fully aware that his feelings of inferiority were promoting his jealousy, Jacob was understandably eager to assert his authority over Esau and rid himself of these feelings once and for all.

But Jacob failed to realize that God would bring about the fulfillment of the promise in His own time. Lacking a sense of God's role in the situation, Jacob took it upon himself to "make things happen"; by taking the matter into his own hands, Jacob was acting as if everything depended on him. Because he was tired

105

of feeling inferior to Esau, Jacob took control and tried to actualize God's promise through deception.

The moment Jacob obtained his father's blessing, his feelings of inferiority turned into feelings of superiority, and his struggle with jealousy completely disappeared. Relying on Rebekah had absolved him from all responsibility, and relying on God's promise had provided the perfect solution — or so he thought. But feeling superior was — in a certain sense — just as bad as feeling inferior; Jacob, like many other introverts, had yet to discover that something more than simply manipulating and controlling external circumstances is required.

This naive trickster was himself tricked by his failure to distinguish between moral and immoral acts: if Jacob was ever to grow up and become a person in his own right, he would have to develop a conscience of his own. Only by coming into his own would it be possible for him to acquire enough respect for others to overcome his unconscious tendency to manipulate and control them. Moreover, without getting more in touch with himself, he would be unable to distinguish between rashness and courage or between cowardice and fear (see figure 19, page 62) — something that is very important for introverts who are beginning to express more of their own individuality.

When Esau discovered that Jacob had obtained the blessing reserved for him, he decided to kill Jacob. Again, Rebekah took the initiative and urged Jacob to flee to her brother's home in Haran. With his mother's assurance that he could return as soon as his brother's fury subsided, Jacob embarked on his journey.

At this point, Jacob must have had trouble believing that God's promises would be fulfilled — they certainly weren't taking place immediately. All that Jacob saw looming before him were the hardships of a long and hazardous journey for which he — the quiet introvert — had no natural inclination, or even aptitude. Resisting the temptation of thinking that an all-out battle with Esau would make a man of him, he used common sense and recognized that to leave would be in the best interest of all — even if it gave the impression that Esau had won again. There was only one advantage as far as Jacob was concerned — at least he would be staying with relatives.

But we are getting a bit ahead of ourselves; let's return to Esau. Jacob had no sooner obtained his father's blessing than Esau returned with the game he had cooked for Isaac.

> His father Isaac asked him, "Who are you?" "I am your first-born son, Esau," he replied. At this Isaac was seized with a great trembling and said, "Who was it, then, that went hunting and brought me game? Unsuspecting I ate before you came; I blessed him, and blessed he will remain!"
>
> (Gen. 27:32-33)

Isaac's trembling indicated how deeply he was affected by what had just happened. His blessing had involved the transferal of special promises made to him by God and to his father Abraham before him; something much more than material blessings was involved here. It was clear that Isaac saw God's hand at work in spite of the deception.

> When Esau heard his father's words, he cried out loudly and bitterly to his father, "Father, bless me too! . . . . have you not saved a blessing for me?" Isaac answered Esau, "See, I have made him your master; I have given him all his brothers as servants, I have provided him with grain and wine. What can I do for you, my son?"
>
> (Gen. 27:34-37)

It is easy to see how heart-rending this was for Isaac because Esau was his favorite son. In one blinding flash, he became aware of his previous insensitivity to his younger son, Jacob, and how God's justice and mercy encompassed both of his sons. Isaac realized that God's will must prevail in spite of his compassion for Esau, but he knew that Esau was not capable of understanding that now. For the first time, Isaac was loving his favorite son in a way that caused him pain. Although Esau was suffering, his father realized it was a necessary suffering.

> Isaac remained silent, and Esau burst into tears.
> Then his father Isaac gave him this answer:
> > "Far from the richness of the earth
> > shall be your dwelling-place,
> > far from the dew that falls from heaven.
> > You shall live by your sword,
> > and you shall serve your brother.

But when you win your freedom, you shall shake his
yoke from your neck."

(Gen. 27:39-40)

What a psychic upheaval for Esau! Nothing could have devastated him more than this apparent reversal in his father's attitude. Esau wasn't the type to admit dependence, but in this blinding instant, he realized how much he had depended on his father and on all the privileges automatically bestowed on the first-born son. He also realized how much of his self-confidence was based on things he had always taken for granted and how little he had appreciated them until now. All the props were pulled out from under him, and he was close to despair. At the very moment when Isaac was affirming Jacob, Esau's weakness was unveiled before his father, and the reversal was too much for the eldest son to bear.

Esau hated Jacob because of the blessing his father had given him and decided to kill his brother as soon as Isaac passed away. No wonder Esau was in a state of shock; he had never really respected Jacob and had never even taken the time to consider his feelings. When he suddenly found himself in a position of being ruled over by his younger brother, he couldn't handle it. Instead of channeling his anger constructively, he let it turn into rashness.

Each brother was driven to rash behavior for very different reasons. The introverted Jacob, feeling the need to assert himself, was trying to rid himself of inferiority feelings through deception, whereas the extraverted Esau, accustomed as he was to taking his father's favor for granted, felt the need to retain it — even if it meant killing his brother. Neither one was concerned with the morality of his actions, but in both instances, the lack of moral conviction reinforced destructive psychological tendencies — in Jacob's case, an overdependence on his mother, and in Esau's case, a blinding drive to upstage his brother. The story of Jacob and Esau not only illustrates the different obstacles that the introvert and extravert encounter in their psychological and moral development, but it also demonstrates how the lack of moral principles can retard psychological growth.

VII

SYMBOLIC IMAGES

WHEN WE TOUCH upon the symbolic dimension of reality, we are left with a sense of being grasped by something much bigger than we are. This "something" has the capacity to grip our whole person. Symbolic experience has the power to stir the creative imagination; it gives birth to insight and deepens understanding.

It is good for us to have some idea of what a symbolic image is all about. Otherwise we are at the mercy of a completely unbridled imagination, floundering on a sea of free-floating images. That is why I have saved this part until last. Much of what I have written so far has been to prepare you for a fuller appreciation of symbolic images.

Symbolic images often leave us feeling a bit insecure and mystified at first, as if we are on foreign territory. Only gradually do we learn to relax and feel comfortable with this kind of experience; it has to be cultivated like an appreciation for art or music. The symbolic image encompasses a reality that is broader and richer than hard facts. A symbol cannot be approached in the same way as a math problem. It doesn't work.

Once we have been gripped by a symbolic experience, the image returns again and again, always revealing something that didn't strike us in quite the same way as it did before. See if this isn't true for you after reading "Children of the Sky" and "Children of the Sea." The first describes an extravert adolescent and the second, an introvert adolescent.

Children of the Sky

Sky children are like birds; they have wings and are most at home in flight. The limitless sky is their father who beckons them beyond all boundaries to an elusive freedom. The earth is their poor mother who clips the wings of their expansive spirit. She humbles her proud children who soar to the heights and descend to the depths. This is the essential rhythm of their souls.

They are wedded to the wind, who is their partner in the dance of life. They know well his gentle caress and his wild fury. His subtle whisper pervades their spirit; his sudden violence wrenches their soul. Who can fathom such an alluring and tormenting partner? His sweeping gales batter, and his swift gusts delight. To surrender is to be hurled like a feather; to survive, one must learn the precision of the dance.

The language of earth is not rhythmic enough, not sufficiently attuned to the impulsive language of the wind. The song of the bird is subtle, in tune with the vibrations of the elusive. He haunts the woodlands with his pulsating, breath-filled cry of exile.

Like lonely waifs, birds keep aloof from the tedium of earth's complexity. They prefer to elude its systems of weights and measures. No need for them to organize the universe, they are free to dart here and there, to follow whim and fancy. Unfettered by the measured steps of earth, they can choose the lawless freedom of the sky.

Small and fragile, their survival is linked to flight. Ill at ease among the wingless creatures of the earth, their feet are unprepared for mapped-out paths. Their eyes are sharp—alert to avoid the snare; they spy flaws in the conventional. Their strategy is isolation and sometimes protest. Rarely announcing their arrival, they perch briefly and are gone.

Children of two worlds, they find no lasting home here. Each year they build their nests anew. Instinct surges as aggressive beaks eagerly gather straw to weave a nurturing circle for their young. The nest betrays the secret of their desperate yearning to make peace with their earth mother.

The springtime ritual reconciles them once again with their humble earth mother. Unable to be contained by the sky, they are compelled to return—dispersed and inflated from their journey—to perpetuate the ritual of maternal containment. Once again fragile balls of fuzz peck their way out of the shell and bask in the enchantment of the maternal nest. The memory of this fleeting paradise lives on as the fledglings spread their wings and respond to the call of the limitless sky.

Children of the Sea

Children of the sea are like shellfish born within the womblike turbulence of the sea. With eyes ceaselessly open to the resurgence of its primordial waters, these children need the protection of their shell.

At first their soft, tender bodies content themselves within the confines of their hard, cumbersome shells. But soon these children begin to notice how awkward and slow-growing they are. They become filled with envy as they watch their more agile, graceful, and swift-moving neighbors. They are tempted at times to fling off their burdensome, "falsifying" shells and surrender their soft, tender bodies unresistingly to the maternal womb of the sea. These children are torn with ambivalence engendered by their constricting shells and the dominance of the sea.

Hard and rigid on the outside, soft and delicate on the inside, they often come close to despairing of their plight. But to no avail. They are left to incubate within their cold, damp, dark shell—yet not without a certain sense of snug, smug security.

One day, it happened that a certain privileged child of the sea caught a glimpse of the serene light of the moon. And as a moonbeam danced on the surface of the waters, it seemed to chant a rhythmic incantation: "The moon is mistress of the sea. Surrender to her tides, surrender to her tides."

From that moment on, the child of the sea entrusted his fate to the serene and beautiful moon, queen of the sea. Whirlpools of ambivalence no longer spun him around the whims and fancies of his capricious sea mother. Eddies of resistance no longer deterred him. Now he moved confidently through the turbulence of the sea with a sense of his destiny being ordained by the gods.

Early one morning, just at the break of dawn, the tides washed him up on a sparkling white beach. How soft and luxurious the sand was! He whispered a greeting to the sweet earth, and peacefully slept in the warm and tender caress of its sand.

111

On awakening, his glance fell upon magnificent shells on the beach. Their delicate colors and masterful etchings ravished his soul. "Perhaps my shell is beautiful, too, and I never knew it!" he exclaimed.

This privileged child of the sea breathed a prayer of gratitude to the mistress of the sea who had brought him safely to this place where the waves washed the face of the soft virgin beach. Then he began to sing with full voice in grateful celebration for life. And as he sang, he lifted his eyes to heaven and began to dance in the moonlight. The time for spawning had come.

The next symbolic image provides both a structural and dynamic model for understanding the dynamics of introversion and extraversion. The cycle of the seasons with their fluctuating rhythms of light and darkness seems the best of all analogies for introversion and extraversion. Extraversion (day-consciousness) and introversion (night-consciousness) clearly dominate certain phases of the yearly cycle. Just as the length of day and night varies during different seasons of the year, extraversion and introversion weave themselves into the fabric of everyone's life.

We've all heard people say "I'm a night person"—meaning that they are wide awake and at their best as the evening wears on. Others claim that they are day people—meaning that they rise early and have the most energy in the morning.

It's the same with personality types. Extraverts, introverts, and ambiverts all start off at different phases of the yearly cycle (see figure 25). The ambivert cycle initiates the movement of the seasons starting with the first day of spring when day and night are exactly equal (point A on chart); it moves through spring into early summer, when the days are longest. The extravert cycle begins during the hottest part of the summer when the days are already beginning to grow shorter, and it moves on through late summer into autumn as night gradually gains greater ascendancy (see point B). The introvert cycle commences when the dominance of night is already clearly established so that introverts settle down to weather the coldest and darkest of all the seasons (refer to point C), in which there is only a faint glimmer of the promise of spring. (This is not to say that ambiverts, extraverts, and introverts are born during these particular seasons—that is obviously not the case.)

INTROVERSION EXTRAVERSION

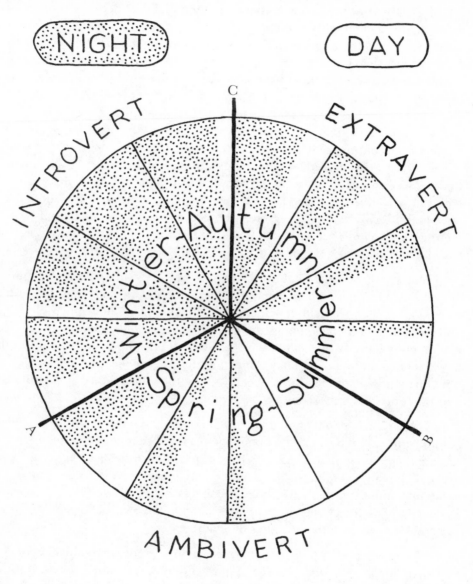

Figure 25

Each type corresponds to a particular seasonal dominance through which the other seasons gain admittance during the course of a person's lifetime. This seasonal dominance, or type, initiates the first phase of development and provides the individual with a sense of identity that ordinarily undergoes various transformations during adolescence and again during the mid-life crisis. During these rites of passage, each person has the opportunity to expand and deepen his consciousness as he continues his journey around the circle (see figure 25). Each of the three major segments of the circle not only represents a different personality type but also represents a different phase of development. Keeping in mind that the personality type always corresponds to the first phase of development, the second phase of growth begins at adolescence and terminates at the mid-life crisis, which initiates the third and final phase. Ordinarily, the latter two phases are somewhat muted by the natural dominance of the personality type into which they are integrated. There is a springtime and a summer, an autumn and a winter, for everyone who actualizes his own potential by completing his cycle of growth; the "self" represents the fully developed and transformed personality type that embraces all four seasons of the year.

During the transition into each new phase of growth, a gradual but nonetheless dramatic change in psychic energy occurs; at each new juncture, the individual experiences a kind of identity crisis. As certain interests begin to fade and lose much of their previous lustre, new ones gradually emerge to take their place; motivation dwindles and tends to slacken off, and people often feel they have reached an impasse. They are aware that their energy levels are shifting, but don't know where the shift will carry them; these new directions are unclear, and the future seems foreboding.

It's not a matter of assuming a new personality type and leaving the old one behind; rather, each transition opens the personality type to assimilate and integrate a new stage of growth, much as a sponge absorbs water. No one could grasp all possible viewpoints at once or deal with the entire range of emotional experience simultaneously without being overwhelmed. Everything takes time. Each new phase of growth incorporates new dimensions of consciousness that previouly hovered on the outskirts of awareness.

The seasonal dominance that symbolizes different personality types is obviously related to the main source of heat and light, the sun. Just as the sun is closest to the horizon in the winter, the more impassioned introvert is closer to

114

the source of his emotions than the extravert. However, during the winter, many of the sun's rays are blocked because they are slanted and have to pass through so much atmosphere (this corresponds to the introvert's somewhat indirect reflective approach to experience).

Extraverts exhibit the versatility and creative tension that one might expect of those whose identity is established in the transition between summer and autumn. Although extraverts begin in the exuberance of summer and enjoy the fruits of its harvest, they are keenly aware that they are moving toward the bleakness of autumn, when plants and trees suddenly shed their bright foliage and die. It's no wonder that they are prone to such abrupt fluctuations in mood and experience a sharp contrast between their naturally dominant extraversion and their less develped introverted side. Extraverts who are about to move into late autumn and on into winter are often convinced that they are introverts because their introversion is becoming increasingly more dominant.

Introverts go through an extensive incubation period during the long, cold winter by keeping cozy and warm at the hearth of a close relationship with their parents. Because of this over-identification, which occurs during the season when darkness triumphs over light, introverts are awakened by the serene radiance of the moon long before their eyes ever catch a glimpse of the sun, and they soon become accustomed to a kind of night vision. The moon illumines the night with a very different beauty than that of the sun, for it depends on the sun for its light, just as young introverts depend on their parents to enlighten them. Extraverts, oblivious to the vista of the night sky, are first awakened by the blinding glare of the noonday sun.

Introverted ambiverts awaken in the early spring when days (extraverted consciousness) and nights (introverted consciousness) are perfectly balanced, when moderate temperatures prevail and the sun is at a medium position in the sky. They counteract the backward pull toward the dark night of over-identification by pressing onward toward continually increasing periods of daylight. Extraverted ambiverts awaken when trees and flowers are already in bud, and when the days are obviously becoming longer than the nights; consequently, as they move from late spring into early summer, they are ready to embark on the extravert phase of development (see figure 25, page 113).

There is a sense in which the ambivert personality is the most desirable

115

because it embodies the most natural pattern of growth. Following the natural progression, everyone passes through the ambivert phase first, the extravert phase second, and the introvert phase last, but when an extravert or an introvert passes through the ambivert phase during latency, it doesn't "take" in the same way that it does for an ambivert.

Since the extravert's deepest experience of himself is rooted in the instinctual and emotional reactions that intruded and interfered with his ability to concentrate during latency, he has to wait until adolescence, which initiates the second and extravert phase of development, when he can identify with others his own age who are also struggling with their instincts and emotions.

The introvert's deepest experience of himself is so bound up with his parents that he passes through latency seeking whatever security he can find, but without really developing a sense of himself as an independent person. Even during adolescence when the introvert approaches the extravert phase, he isn't ready to deal directly with his instincts and emotions; he feels more comfortable transferring his emotional attachment from his parents to a prospective marriage partner. Only as the introvert approaches the mid-life crisis — which initiates the third and introvert phase of development — can he really identify with those extraverts and ambiverts who are now seeking to understand the deeper, more fundamental meaning of life. This is not to say that the different facets of the previous phases completely escaped his consciousness — only that the soil was not rich and deep enough for him to root his identity there.

None of the personality types fully actualize themselves until they have encompassed all three phases of development. It's natural for ambiverts to settle into the ambivert phase just as the extraverts tend to settle into the extravert phase — and not move on. Consequently, the advantage that ambiverts and extraverts have in the beginning often balances out in the end as the slow and steady introverts continually plod toward the finish line — as in the fable of "The Tortoise and the Hare."

Since the types exist along a continuum in which each third of the circle also represents a phase of development (see figure 25, page 113), people who establish an identity near the boundary between two different types are usually more affected by the dynamics of their transitional position than by the prominence of one type or the other. It is difficult for them to determine which type is

116

more dominant, simply because they are constantly shifting back and forth between the dynamics of both. Because transitional dynamics are more fluid than type dynamics, these people tend to float along until they discover which type really grounds them in a sense of who they are. It is their awareness of being torn for most of their lives between two conflicting sets of dynamics — both of which are partially conscious — that distinguishes them from those who try to ignore the natural dynamics of their type in favor of another. Such a futile attempt at imitation is most likely to occur in the introvert in our society where extraversion is so highly valued (it is just the opposite in the Orient where introversion is held in higher esteem). However, when those who find themselves on the boundary between two types discover their more dominant type, they are in a better position to deal with the transitional dynamics that move them from one phase of growth to another, thus enabling them to better integrate the dynamics of the less dominant type.

Sometimes extraverts concentrate entirely on the shaded or introverted dimension of their personality, just as introverts often concentrate on the unshaded or extraverted dimension of their type (see figure 25, page 113). When this tendency develops we have the phenomena of the uncomfortably quiet extravert, who feels a bit constricted, and the overly talkative introvert, who is somewhat dispersed. In such instances, observers almost always get the impression that the extravert is "bottled up" and that the introvert is a bit "too much." This is probably what Jung meant when he referred to inferior introversion in the extravert and inferior extraversion in the introvert. On the other hand, when an extravert focuses completely on the unshaded or extraverted dimension of his personality type, his natural expansion turns into dispersion (see figure 15, page 48). Similarly, when an introvert focuses entirely on the shaded or introverted dimension of his type, his natural contraction turns into constriction (see figure 17, page 52). Thus we see that the concept of personality types admits of an almost infinite number of variations.

When introverts, extraverts, and ambiverts concentrate on the dynamic combination of introversion and extraversion within their respective types, we can speak of a kind of ambiversion that is available to all personality types. Just as the shaded portions represent introversion, or night consciousness, and the unshaded portions represent extraversion, or day consciousness (both of which occur throughout the entire cycle), so too we can speak of ambiversion whenever an individual integrates both dimensions wherever he happens to be in his journey around the circle of life. Although the quality of the ambiversion is obviously related to its location within the cycle, it can be recognized by the habitual awareness of both the introverted and extraverted dimensions of consciousness that is linked to a particular phase of development.

Thus we can make a distinction between the terms introvert, extravert, and ambivert, which refer to the structural aspects of the model, and the terms introversion, extraversion, and ambiversion, which refer to the dynamic aspects of the model.

Keeping in mind how the differing lengths of days and nights are woven into the rhythm of the seasons, one can detect both a major and minor theme in the orchestration of an essentially archetypal symbol that incorporates both structural and dynamic dimensions. The major theme corresponds to the particular seasonal dominance that represents the structure of different personality types, whereas the minor theme represents the dynamic way in which introversion, extraversion, and ambiversion weave themselves into all the personality types throughout the entire life cycle. Viewing the model as a whole enables one to see how intimately the major and minor themes are interrelated. This model also has the advantage of being able to illustrate the relationship of each personality type to the whole spectrum of potential consciousness—which represents the "self."

The development of the natural moral virtues—if understood in relation to the structure of personality types and their dynamic cycle of movement around the circle through the various developmental phases—enables us to achieve the integration that is essential to actualize the self. By providing a kind of advance preparation that helps us through the difficult periods of transition in our lives, the virtues keep us from being completely determined by the conditioning of our early childhood experience and by the limitations of our own subjective consciousness at a given point in time. The virtues direct our energies in ways that benefit the whole self—encompassing the entire cycle from birth to death—by keeping us from getting locked into a particular phase of development. Relating the natural moral virtues to a model of the human psyche that embraces both structural and dynamic components enables us to obtain the self-knowledge we need if the Spirit is to become a vital and dynamic force in our lives.

A NOTE

Sister Reardon has conducted a series of workshops under the general heading of Understanding Ourselves and Our Children. *The whole project developed as a result of her study during the past ten years of Jungian psychology, concentrating particularly upon the dynamics of different personality types as they evolve during childhood and adolescence and on through adult life.*

In the workshops, as in this book, Sister Reardon describes how most interpersonal conflicts, whether they are between husband and wife, parent and child, or friends, are related to differences in personality types that need to be recognized and understood. She also shows how the flowering of virtue, which is so intimately related to the unfolding of the human personality, can help to bridge these differences.

Personality and Morality: A Developmental Approach *evolved along with Sister Reardon's experiences in giving the workshops. She had become increasingly aware of the problems created by the departmentalization of the psychological and spiritual aspects of life. It was her desire to restore the relationship between the two that resulted in both the book and the workshops. By relating the contrasting dynamics of personality types to examples from Scripture, the workshops challenge those who attend to integrate the spiritual and psychological dimensions of their lives.*

For more information concerning the workshops, please.contact the publisher.

BIBLIOGRAPHY

This bibliography is limited only to the works that have had the greatest bearing upon the evolution of my thought.

ALLPORT, GORDON. *Becoming: Basic Considerations for a Psychology of Personality.* New Haven: Yale University Press, 1955.

BRENNAN, ROBERT E. *The Seven Horns of the Lamb.* Milwaukee: Bruce Publishing Company, 1966 (I have used Brennan's interpretation of Thomas Aquinas throughout this volume.)

DETLOFF, WAYNE, "Psychological Types: Fifty Years After," *Psychological Perspectives,* III (Spring, 1972), 62-73.

ERIKSON, ERIK. *Childhood and Society.* New York: W.W. Norton, 1950.

_____. *Identity, Youth and Crisis.* New York: W.W. Norton, 1965.

GRAY, HORACE. "Psychological Types and Changes with Age," *Journal of Clinical Psychology,* III (July, 1947), 273-277.

GRAY, HORACE, AND WHEELWRIGHT, JOSEPH B., M.D., "Jung's Psychological Types and Marriage," *Stanford Medical Bulletin,* II No. 1 (February 1944), 37-39.

GREENE, THAYER. "Confessions of an Extravert," *Quadrant,* VIII (Winter, 1975), 21-31.

HILLMAN, JAMES. "Types, Images and the Perception of Uniqueness," (lectures delivered in New York City, January 23-24, 1977), 2 reels. New York: C.G. Jung Foundation for Analytical Psychology.

Jerusalem Bible, The. Reader's Edition. New York: Doubleday and Company, Inc., 1968.

JUNG, CARL G. *Memories, Dreams, Reflections.* New York: Vintage Books, 1965.

_____. *Psychological Types.* Princeton: Princeton University Press, 1971.

_____. *Two Essays on Analytical Psychology.* Princeton: Princeton University Press, 1966.

KOHLBERG, LAWRENCE. "Collected Papers on Moral Development and Moral Education," privately printed, 1973.

LAING, RONALD D. *The Divided Self.* Baltimore: Pelican, 1965.

LUIJPEN, W. *Existential Phenomenology.* Pittsburgh: Duquesne University Press, 1969.

MAY, ROLLO. *Love and Will.* New York: Basic Books, 1970.

MILLER, DONALD E. *The Wing-Footed Wanderer.* Nashville: Abingdon Press, 1977.

MYERS, ISABEL BRIGGS, AND MYERS, PETER B. *Gifts Differing.* Palo Alto: Consulting Psychologist Press, 1980.

NEUMANN, ERICH. *The Child.* New York: G.P. Putnam's Sons, 1973.

ORNSTEIN, ROBERT E. (ed.). *The Nature of Human Consciousness.* New York: Viking Press, 1974.

PIAGET, JEAN. *The Moral Judgment of the Child.* New York: MacMillan, 1955.

_____. *Structuralism.* New York: Basic Books, 1970.

SHAPIRO, KENNETH J. "A Critique of Introversion," *Spring,* (1972).

SHAPIRO, KENNETH J., AND ALEXANDER, IRVING E. *The Experience of Introversion.* Durham: Duke University Press, 1975.

_____. "Extraversion-Introversion, Affiliation, and Anxiety," *Journal of Personality,* XXXVII (1969), 387-406.

VON FRANZ, MARIE LOUISE, AND HILLMAN, JAMES. *Jung's Typology.* Zurich: Spring Publications, 1971.

WHEELWRIGHT, JOSEPH, M.D. "Psychological Types," a monograph. San Francisco: C.G. Jung Institute of San Francisco, 1973.

WHEELWRIGHT, JOSEPH B., M.D., WHEELWRIGHT, JANE H., BUEHLER, JOHN A., M.D., PH.D. "Jungian Type Survey: The Gray-Wheelwrights Test," (16th Revision). Society of Jungian Analysts of Northern California, 1964.